PRAISE FOR **BURN YOUR MORTGAGE**

"Sean's personal journey to financial freedom is a brave and inspiring one, and I am delighted to see him share his learning with the world. *Burn Your Mortgage* offers practical, clear and useful insights to help people of all walks of life live healthier financial lives. I am convinced that *Burn Your Mortgage* is set to be a pivotal guidebook to achieving financial freedom."

Peter Aceto, President and CEO, Tangerine

"A home is the largest purchase most people make, yet there is little information to help them make smart choices. Most advice comes from banks, mortgage brokers, real estate agents, lawyers and home inspectors—not exactly objective. I'm glad to see Sean Cooper use his experience as home buyer, mortgage burner, landlord and freelance writer to guide others through the steps to take to come out ahead in the real estate game."

Ellen Roseman, *Toronto Star* columnist, University of Toronto continuing education instructor and *Canadian MoneySaver* contributor

"A clear and concise plan for millennials looking for a path to financial independence early in their career."

Don R. Campbell, bestselling author of *Real Estate Investing in Canada*, frequent guest on the Business News Network

"Chock-full of actionable tips based on real life experience, Sean Cooper's *Burn Your Mortgage* is a valuable resource for anyone considering buying a home in Canada. In more than just another mortgage manual, Sean writes passionately about the pitfalls to avoid during the house-buying process and then, with equal passion, shows you how to achieve an important step toward financial freedom by paying off your mortgage as quickly as possible."

Robert R. Brown, author of *Wealthing Like Rabbits: An Original Introduction to Personal Finance*, and *MoneySense* columnist

D1373484

"*Burn Your Mortgage* will push you just outside your comfort zone—which is exactly what you need to really make progress on your mortgage. Sean Cooper walks the talk. His obsession with frugal living provides a ton of great lessons on how to get ahead financially."

Bruce Sellery, bestselling author of *Moolala*, personal finance expert for *Cityline* and *MoneySense*

"Sean has written an invaluable book. He paid off his mortgage before 31, achieved financial freedom, and shares his entire journey, step by step, so you can too. The chapters on turning your home into an income source and generating 'side hustle' income alone are worth the price of *Burn Your Mortgage*. A great addition to personal finance literature and a must-read if you want to build wealth."

Robin R. Speziale, bestselling author of *Market Masters*

"*Burn Your Mortgage* offers solid advice, tested by personal experience, for a generation that feels rising house prices have put homeownership out of reach. Sean Cooper encourages people to focus on what's possible, and set goals to make homeownership a reality."

Peter Mitham, co-author of *Real Estate Investing for Canadians for Dummies* and real estate columnist for *Business in Vancouver*

"He may be the millennial man who riled the Internet by paying off his mortgage, but Sean Cooper offers concrete suggestions for owning your concrete quickly. In *Burn Your Mortgage* he shares the financial priorities, choices, and trade-offs he made to be mortgage-free fast. Following even a few of his frugal ways will get you to homeowner status sooner."

Kerry K. Taylor, Squawkfox.com, author of *397 Ways to Save Money*

"Few weekend tennis players would want to train like Serena Williams. That would involve a lot of sacrifice. But could a weekend racket warrior learn from Serena? Absolutely. I would say the same thing, for the same reasons, about Sean Cooper's obsession to pay off his mortgage. *Burn Your Mortgage* describes his groundstrokes well."

Andrew Hallam, author of *Millionaire Teacher: The Nine Rules of Wealth You Should Have Learned in School*, 2nd edition

"With the high price of Canadian housing, many millennials fear they can never own a home. Sean Cooper is one millennial who shows them how they can, based on his own experiences with frugality, landlording and shrewd investing. Cooper covers all the bases and shows how the foundation of financial independence is still a paid-for home."

Jonathan Chevreau, co-author of *Victory Lap Retirement*, columnist for the *Financial Post* and *MoneySense*, and founder of the Financial Independence Hub

"Excellent! Packed with powerful, practical ideas, this inspiring book will help any Canadian own a home faster, become debt-free, and achieve financial freedom. I highly recommend buying a copy for yourself if you're not retired, and if you are, gifting it to your kids."

Talbot Stevens, speaker and author of *The Smart Debt Coach*

"Regardless of your opinion on extreme frugality, I think we can all agree that setting financial goals and proactively pursuing them helps keep you honest about your finances. Whether it's paying off debt or planning for retirement, you can't be an ostrich with your head in the ground. Sean's motivational story and the advice he shares in this book can help you burn your mortgage—and if you're already debt-free, it can help reinforce the importance of being financially accountable to yourself."

Jason Heath, fee-only financial planner and personal finance columnist for the *Financial Post* and *MoneySense* magazine

"Simple, yet effective advice. I highly recommend these strategies!"

Derek Foster, author of *The Idiot Millionaire*

"I thoroughly enjoyed *Burn Your Mortgage*. Sean provides all of the detailed information required to purchase your home and get rid of the mortgage fast."

Ross Grant, author of *Destination: Early Financial Independence*

"A must-read guide. Frugality tips at their best."

Rahim Madhavji, investment banker, entrepreneur, guest contributor on BNN, and President of KnightsbridgeFX

"Through frugal and balanced living, Sean Cooper paid off his mortgage decades sooner than most Canadians, and he achieved this milestone on a five-figure salary. *Burn Your Mortgage* is packed with practical and inspiring strategies to become a super-saver and crush your mortgage. Mr. Cooper's tips won't leave you eating baked beans and Kraft Dinner. Rather, they're suited to your income and lifestyle. This a must-read for 20-something Canadians who believe in the dream of owning their own home and building wealth through real estate."

Lesley-Anne Scorgie, bestselling author, CBC financial expert and founder of MeVest

"Before you start into the home-buying process, buy this book. In an easy style, Sean leads you through the experience, leaving you informed and prepared. Sean has done his research and offers honest and valuable tips that will save the homeowner money not only on their initial purchase, but for managing financial responsibilities and challenges over the life of the mortgage. This truly is an insider's guide so you can make informed decisions and alleviate some of the anxiety that goes along with buying a house.

Som Seif, President & CEO, Purpose Investments Inc., and guest contributor on BNN, on CBC and for the *Financial Post*

Moran,
Happy mortgage burning!
S Cooper

Burn Your Mortgage

THE SIMPLE,

POWERFUL

PATH TO

FINANCIAL

FREEDOM FOR

CANADIANS

Sean Cooper

BURN YOUR MORT-GAGE

COPPER COIN

Copper Coin
Toronto, Canada

Cataloguing in Publication Data available
from Library and Archives Canada
ISBN 978-0-9952029-0-0 (paperback)
ISBN 978-0-9952029-1-7 (ebook)

Cover and text design by Peter Cocking
Printed and bound in Canada

17 18 19 20 21   5 4 3 2 1

Contents

Part 2 **The Buy**

Part 3 **Congratulations, You're a Homeowner! Now What?**

Author's Note
The Mortgage-Burning Party

"**D**ING-DONG, THE mortgage is dead," I triumphantly announced as I set fire to my mortgage in front of my cheering family and friends outside a pub in the heart of downtown Toronto. The three-year journey to mortgage freedom was finally over.

At the ripe old age of 27, I had bought my first house. It's a beautifully renovated three-bedroom bungalow in Toronto, Canada's second most expensive housing market, where the average detached house goes for over $1 million. I purchased my house for $425,000, which was a bargain. I was thrilled to finally be able to call myself a home-owner. It had taken me over two years of house hunting and two failed offers to find a place I could call my own. All my hard work and frugal living had paid off. I made a sizable down payment of $170,000, leaving me with a mortgage of $255,000.

Six figures of debt—slightly over a quarter of a million dollars—is pretty intimidating, especially when just one person is carrying it, so I made a plan to pay down my mortgage as quickly as possible. I chose a five-year fixed-rate mortgage at 3.04%.

Melissa Leong of the *Financial Post*, Canada's business newspaper, wrote about my ambitious plan to be mortgage-free. She talked about my single-minded path to debt freedom, which included living in the basement of my new house while tenants thumped around upstairs. Managing to pay off over $100,000 of my mortgage in a year and half, I could taste mortgage freedom.

The journey toward mortgage freedom wasn't easy. Between my two jobs as a senior pension analyst and a personal finance journalist, I typically worked up to 80 hours a week, putting every spare penny toward my mortgage. I was careful with my travel budget but still managed to have fun. I didn't take extravagant vacations but instead did daytrips to Niagara Falls and went camping. I was diligent and dedicated. I watched my spending on clothing, entertainment and dining out. I made paying off my mortgage my top priority. Basically, I ate, breathed and slept my mortgage.

Some people have questioned my lifestyle choice. Yes, I could have done a better job of achieving work-life balance, but I see it as short-term pain for long-term gain. I may have worked very hard for three years, but now I have the rest of my life to enjoy, without a massive mortgage holding me back.

SEPTEMBER 22 WILL forever be a date etched in my memory, for it's the date I paid off my mortgage. I managed to pay it off in three years and two months, ahead of schedule, and before turning 31.

To celebrate, I threw a mortgage-burning party to thank my family and friends for their support (burning the mortgage papers is an old tradition for homeowners who've paid off their home). After living conservatively, I went all out. I spent hundreds of dollars on a new suit and on hosting the party—I wanted it to be the mortgage-burning party for the ages. I invited the CBC to film the big moment when my mortgage papers went up in flames.

I had prepared a speech in which I talked about how I hadn't taken any shortcuts in paying off my mortgage, joking that didn't have a trust account the size of Paris Hilton's. My mother was the inspiration for my paying down my mortgage so quickly. When she was downsized during the dot-com bubble, she struggled as a single mother to pay the mortgage and raise two children. Seeing what she went through, I vowed to pay down my mortgage as soon as possible. I lightheartedly remarked that it would be the most important day of my life—until my wedding.

After delivering my speech, with friends and CBC reporter Sophia Harris waiting in anticipation, I attempted to set fire to my mortgage papers. Things didn't go as planned—for five minutes I tried unsuccessfully to light the papers. Finally they caught fire and went up in flames. I felt like the weight of the world was lifted off my shoulders. This, I thought, is what mortgage freedom feels like.

My story aired on CBC's *The National*. Thanks to a stroke of luck and good timing, the story went viral. I received coverage in all the major media outlets in Canada: CBC, CTV, BNN, Global TV, the *Globe and Mail* and the *Toronto Star*. My story made headlines around the world. I was featured in the U.K.'s *Daily Mail* tabloid and appeared on Australia's top-rated breakfast show, *Sunrise*. In the U.S., I filmed a segment for *Good Morning America* and was a guest on Dave Ramsey's syndicated radio show.

Although I garnered a lot of attention from the media, it wasn't all good publicity. I was painted as a frugal extremist—someone who lived like a pauper, eating Kraft Dinner for every meal and never going out with friends. I do enjoy Kraft Dinner on occasion, but that particular portrayal of me couldn't be further from the truth. I'm just a regular, fun-loving person. When I'm not working, I enjoy catching up with friends, cycling, weightlifting, public speaking, cooking and creative writing. And I'm not ashamed to admit I'm a bit of a nerd—I'm a big fan of *Chicago P.D.*, *Law & Order* and *Star Wars*. And I'm relentless in achieving my goals.

My story is polarizing. Some people think I did a great thing; other people, not so much. You be the judge. Here are comments I received on a CBC News story:

> Upstanding citizen works his life away, lives in miserable squalor and forgoes human relationships for years. How is this an inspirational story?

> Yet another privileged white man bragging about how he "did it on his own." But did anyone notice how big his down payment was? Or the fact that he has a $75K+ full-time job?

I get where these people are coming from. Paying off your mortgage in three years is probably not realistic for most people. The good news is that you don't have to pay off your mortgage in *my* timeline. My story may be exceptional, but hopefully you can draw inspiration from it. If I can pay off my mortgage so quickly, you too can do it faster and sooner than you imagine. And you don't have to ditch your friends, eat only Kraft Dinner and go to financial extremes to pay off your mortgage sooner.

Most personal finance books tell you to get rid of the small things in life—usually the things that make you happy. My message is different: you can still enjoy the finer things in life like a Starbucks coffee or an iPhone (within reason), you just have to be smart on the big purchases like a home or car. You don't have to give up travelling, say, but you do need to take financial freedom seriously and make it your top priority.

There are simple things you can do in your everyday life to reach mortgage-free financial freedom. In these pages, I provide realistic guidelines you can follow to pay down your mortgage faster. My advice is relevant whether you're single, raising a family, a millennial or part of Gen X.* Instead of paying off your mortgage in 25 years, pay it off at the pace that works for you, whether that's 10, 15 or 20 years. But the sooner, the better.

If owning a home, never mind paying off a huge mortgage, seems intimating, join the club. I felt the same way five years ago. Fast-forward to today and not only do I own a home, but it's paid off. This book serves as a blueprint for anyone who wants to burn their mortgage papers sooner rather than later.

I hope to inspire and motivate you to follow in my footsteps, to apply lessons from my experience to your own journey to mortgage freedom—so that you too can have a mortgage-burning party for the ages.

---

* Millennials are those born between the early 1980s and early 2000s; Gen Xers, those born between the early 1960s and early 1980s.

Introduction
Ending the Mortgage Life Sentence

MANY PEOPLE CONSIDER their mortgage a life sentence. I'm here to tell you that it's not. Many homeowners start with a 25- to 30-year mortgage amortization (how long it will you take to fully repay the mortgage), but there's nothing stopping you from paying your mortgage off sooner. As you'll soon learn, there are many simple things you can do in your everyday life to be mortgage-free.

My aim is to inspire you to grab the mortgage bull by the horns and take control of your finances. This book isn't *just* about buying a home and paying it off sooner; it's about financial freedom. In it I give you the tools you need to rethink how you view money and to reshape your finances. You too can enjoy life without that huge debt hanging over your head.

The Homeownership Dream Is Still Alive and Well

It's hard to read the news these days without seeing a story about real estate. Real estate remains affordable in most cities, though not in Toronto and Vancouver, where the average price of a detached home is over $1 million.

Prime Minister Justin Trudeau hit the nail on the head when he said, "Rising home prices [and] uncertainty around being able to buy your first home or upgrade as you want, to grow a family, is a real drag on our economy and a real drag on Canadians' opportunities."[1] The lack of affordable housing can be discouraging for homebuyers, to say the least. Yet despite all the doom and gloom in the media, two-thirds of millennials still expect to own their own home.[2]

But not every home in Toronto or Vancouver costs over $1 million. Not every home sells in a frenzied bidding war. There are still affordable options. You might not be able to afford a detached house right away, but you could probably swing a condo downtown or a townhouse in the suburbs and start building up equity. Homeownership is alive and well in Canada. It's all about setting realistic expectations.

Your Mortgage Is Your Top Financial Priority

For most people, homeownership is the single biggest financial challenge of their lives. "What if I lose my job and can't pay my mortgage?" is the question keeping many homeowners up at night.

Many people are guilty of buying "too much house"—a home at the top of their price range. Why do banks sign off on the massive mortgages for these properties? Because they know you'll put your mortgage ahead of everything else.

And that makes sense. If you dust off your university psychology textbook and turn to the page explaining Maslow's hierarchy of needs, you'll see that shelter—a physiological need—is among the most important. It's hard to argue with facts: despite record-high household debt levels in Canada, we're still finding a way to make our mortgage payments—delinquency rates on mortgages are near record lows.[3]

If you run into financial problems, you'll keep treating your mortgage as your top priority. You'll get a second job, use your line of credit or make cash advances on your credit card (which, for the record, I don't recommend)—anything to avoid defaulting on your mortgage. The last thing you want is to come home to find a foreclosure notice posted on your front door. You'll keep paying your mortgage so you'll have a roof over your head.

Why Pay Down Your Mortgage
When You Can Come Out Ahead Investing?

Some people have questioned my decision to pay down debt. Since interest rates were near a record low, I shouldn't have been in any hurry to pay down my debt, they say. And with the household debt-to-income ratio near a record high, you may feel this way too. Low interest rates are causing many homeowners to pile on more debt. You don't want to fall into the debt trap. I'll show you how to buck the trend.

If the financial crisis of 2008 has taught us anything, it's that investment returns are far from guaranteed. The uncertainty in the markets has people flocking to the real estate market, pushing home prices well beyond any increases in wages and inflation. Financial advisers may say you can expect a rate of return of 5% or 6% on your investment portfolio, but there's no guarantee you'll get that. That's why I prefer the guaranteed rate of return in paying down my mortgage: I know the rate of return I'm going to get—it's my mortgage rate.

A common argument is that it doesn't make sense to buy a home in a big city. That renting is a lot less expensive and the way to go. As real estate blogger Garth Turner so bluntly put it, "Why would any... person want to buy a condo in Toronto or Calgary or Vancouver and actually pay twice the monthly cost than it would take to rent the same unit?" Kevin O'Leary of ABC's *Shark Tank* shares a similar view. Mr. Wonderful has gone on record saying you'd be an "idiot" to buy a home (I guess I'm king of the idiots, since I not only bought a house in a big city, I paid it off). We're told we'd be better off renting and investing.

When it comes to the performance of real estate versus the stock market, the findings seem to back this up. The average price of a resale home in Canada was up 5.4% from 2004 to 2013. Over the same time, the S&P/TSX Composite Index posted a 7.97% return. It seems pretty clear: you're better off renting and investing than you are buying.

So why isn't the debate over? Because it's flawed. It ignores the power of leverage. *Leverage* is a fancy way of saying you're borrowing the bank's money to invest in something that's expected to go up in value. You're leveraging when the bank lets you borrow up to 95% of a home's value. The bank doesn't let you borrow this much money for stocks. Why not? Because real estate is seen as a safe, long-term investment. (It's also because of collateral. If you lose all your money in the stock market, the bank has nothing, but if you default on your mortgage, the bank can sell your home to recover some or all of its money.) Here's an example that shows the power of leverage: Let's say you bought a home a decade ago for $250,000, with only 10% down ($25,000). You later sold it for $400,000, making $125,000 in profit (for simplicity's sake, we'll ignore associated costs such as mortgage interest, mortgage insurance, property taxes and closing costs). Even though your home only went up in value by 60%, that's a 500% return on your initial investment (down payment) of $25,000. Try finding that kind of return in the stock market!

Risk management is another good reason to pay down debt. Often, a homeowner's biggest fear is losing their job, and jobs are far from guaranteed these days. Globalization means you could show up for work tomorrow to find that your job is being outsourced. If this happens to you, you'll probably wonder how you'll pay your mortgage. You can always stop investing when you lose your job, but if you stop paying your mortgage, not only will you eventually lose your home, you'll also ruin your credit score. It's a double whammy.

The final compelling reason to pay down your mortgage is to *save on interest*. For most families, a mortgage is the largest debt of their lifetime. If you pay off your mortgage sooner, you'll save a boatload in interest. If you buy a $375,000 home with a 10% down payment of $37,500, you'll need a $345,600 mortgage (this includes mortgage insurance of $8,100). If you paid off your mortgage monthly over 25 years at a mortgage rate of 2.99%, you'd pay total interest of $144,529. But if you paid off your mortgage more aggressively, in only 15 years, you'd pay total interest of only $83,146, for a savings of $61,383. Not bad! The higher the mortgage rate, the more advantageous it is to pay off your mortgage sooner.

When you make prepayments on your mortgage, the payments go straight toward principal, saving a ton in interest. If and when interest rates rise, you'll have peace of mind knowing you paid off a large chunk of your mortgage while rates were low. You won't sweat the higher mortgage payments, since you're already used to them.

Average national home sale price · 1980–2015

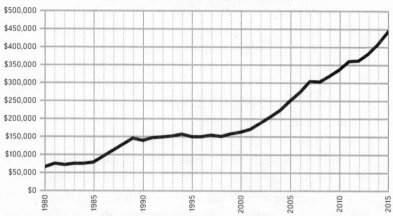

Canadian real estate prices have been trending upward over the past 25 years. That's more than we can say about the stock market over this same time.* *Data source:* CANADIAN REAL ESTATE ASSOCIATION

There are cases where it probably doesn't make sense to rush to pay down your mortgage (e.g., if you have credit card debt or if your employer offers a pension plan with matching contributions), but in many cases, paying off your mortgage sooner *does* make sense.

Could you earn more from investing? Maybe. But if you're anything like me, you may not sleep well as a mortgage holder. And nothing beats a good night's sleep.

Your Journey toward Homeownership and Mortgage Freedom

This book is divided into three parts, each covering an area of your finances to help you own a home and pay it off sooner.

---

* If you're anything like me, your eyes glaze over when you see too many graphs. Enjoy this graph, because it's the only one you'll find in this book.

It's hard to pay off a mortgage if you can't afford a home. Part 1 arms you with the tools you need to set yourself up for financial freedom. It covers everything from goal setting to being thrifty. We'll look at the importance of budgeting and tracking your spending. The biggest hurdle to buying a home is the down payment, so I show you ways to supercharge your savings. If you already own a home, you'll still find plenty of useful savings tips that you can apply to your everyday life to pay off your mortgage sooner.

In Part 2 we dive straight into home buying and mortgages. We'll cover everything you need to know about buying a home so that you'll end up in your dream home with a mortgage you can afford. You'll learn everything you need to know about mortgages, so that you can confidently walk through the doors of your bank (or other lender) in search of a mortgage. I share my secrets on how to burn your mortgage. And because buyers are often blindsided by closing costs, this topic is also looked at.

For most people, their home represents their life savings. Part 3 looks at ways to protect it (including everyone's favourite topic, insurance). In the final chapter I share my secrets of being a successful landlord, so that you too can, in the words of Scott McGillivray from HGTV's *Income Property*, "bring cheques to the bank."

Most of all, I want to inspire you to take action. You can read all the books you want on weight loss and listen to hours of TED Talks, but unless you take action, you won't achieve your goals. To that end, at the end of each chapter you'll find five key mortgage-burning takeaways. Although not all the takeaways speak directly to burning your mortgage, they're important factors to consider in saving for your down payment, buying a house, and achieving financial freedom by paying off your mortgage.

Everyone's financial freedom is different. Your idea of financial freedom might be eventually selling your home and travelling the world, whereas mine might be leaving the corporate world and starting my own business. The bottom line is that a paid-off home gives you options.

So, are you ready for your exciting journey toward homeownership and mortgage freedom? Let's get started!

Part One

Setting Yourself Up for Financial Freedom

Stay focused, go after your dreams
and keep moving toward your goals.
LL COOL J, rapper

1

Goal Setting
The First Step toward a Mortgage-Free Home

I'M FAR FROM perfect. In fact, I struggled throughout high school. I was a mediocre student at best. When most of my classmates were busy working part-time jobs, I spent my time playing video games. After graduating from high school, I hit rock bottom. I was unemployed, living in my mother's basement for almost a year, with a net worth of only $5,000. Getting my first job at age 19 lit a fire under me. After enrolling in college and managing to rack up ten thousand dollars in student loans, I set for myself the ambitious goal of graduating debt-free.

While many fellow students were out enjoying pub nights, I held down three part-time jobs—and managed to get straight As, making the dean's Honour List. And I was thrifty: I purchased my textbooks second-hand, cycled and rode public transit, and packed my lunch. After three years of college and two years of university, I graduated debt-free with a net worth of $70,000.

If I can turn my finances around, so can you. It comes down to two things: goal setting, and working hard to achieve those goals.

Set SMART Goals

I wouldn't be where I am today without the simple yet powerful technique of goal setting. Without goals, you can easily wander around directionless, without a purpose. Setting goals gives you a sense of purpose. You'll feel motivated when you wake up each morning. Goal setting gives you the self-motivation to do what needs to get done to reach your ultimate goals. Goal setting has helped me graduate debt-free from university, buy a home in one of North America's most expensive cities (Toronto) and achieve a net worth of over $500,000 by age 29.

Successful people take goal setting a step further and set *stretch goals*—goals that are difficult but achievable with extra effort. Rapper Drake set the goal of making $25 million by age 25, and guess what? He achieved it. I set the stretch goal of paying off my mortgage by age 31. Not only did I pay off my mortgage, I did it even sooner, by age 30.

And successful people don't stop there. Once they've achieved a goal, they work toward their next goal, a goal that is even bigger. Successful people aren't afraid to dream big. Drake's next goal is, apparently, making $250 million by age 29. My next goal is achieving a net worth of $1 million by age 35 (I know that pales in comparison to Drake, but as I mention later, it's best not to compare oneself to others).

Goal setting is a great start in your quest for financial freedom, but you'll still need to develop an action plan. For doing that, I'm a big fan of SMART goals. "SMART" is an acronym for "**S**pecific, **M**easurable, **A**ttainable, **R**elevant, **T**ime-Bound." Here's an example of a SMART goal:

Specific: I want to purchase a one-bedroom condo in Toronto.
Measurable: I will "pay myself first" by setting up a preauthorized savings plan at my bank.
Attainable: I will save $1,667 per month in a high-interest savings account.
Relevant: By achieving this goal, I can get my foot in the door of the Toronto real estate market and start building equity.
Time-Bound: I will save up a down payment of $60,000 in three years.

What Are Your SMART Goals?

I want you to grab a pen and paper right now and write down your top three goals using the SMART goals framework. Then post that piece of paper somewhere you visit every day. Whether it's near your computer, beside your bed or in the office, it will be a constant reminder of the goals you've set for yourself and how you plan to achieve them. Here's a model to get you started:

Specific:
_____

Measurable:
_____

Attainable:
_____

Relevant:
_____

Time-Bound:
_____

It's our behaviour that stops us from achieving our goals. If we took the time to break down goals into actionable steps, they wouldn't seem so daunting. That glass ceiling? That brass ring? Break it. Take it.

Beat Procrastination

The biggest obstacle to accomplishing your goals is procrastination. Does "Oh, I'll get around to it later" sound familiar? The problem is that "later" often never comes. Unless you make a game plan and follow through with it, you'll likely find yourself in the same place five years later. People tend to procrastinate when it comes to their finances. They'll be super pumped about getting their finances in shape after reading a life-changing personal finance book (*ahem!*) but will then fall into the same old trap once the initial excitement wears off.

In the words of Dr. Phil, "How's that working for you?" You can't expect to accomplish *something* by doing *nothing*. Procrastination is the biggest enemy of success. You don't have to get it perfect, you just have to get it going. Your finances are far too important to put on the back burner. It's time to make your finances a priority today—not tomorrow or next week. You know by now that it's a good idea to budget, buy a home (well, usually) and save for retirement, but have you actually taken the steps to achieve those long-term goals? Make yourself a plan and set goals today. I did, and so can you.

Create a Strong Work Ethic

Setting goals is a good start, but it alone won't get you anywhere. You have to be willing to roll up your sleeves and work hard. I worked between 70 and 80 hours a week while paying down my mortgage. You don't have to work as many hours as me to own a home and pay off your mortgage, but you do have to be willing to do what it takes to achieve both your short-term and long-term goals.

Most successful people possess high levels of energy and try to take advantage of every waking moment. For them, it's not enough to hold down a steady job—they want to achieve more. Successful people are willing to put in the long work hours without breaking a sweat. Work hard, play hard is the motto they live by. It's the desire to succeed coupled with the high level of energy that sets successful people apart from the rest.

Practise Good Time Management

Respected NFL coach George Allen summed up good time management perfectly when he said, "Try not to do too many things at once. Know what you want, the number one thing today and tomorrow. Persevere and get it done."[1] Feeling overwhelmed by having too much to tackle often prevents people from achieving their goals. Staying organized and managing your time wisely are key in achieving your goals. People often ask me how I managed to work several jobs and still have time to cook my meals, pack my lunch and spend time with family and friends. It all came down to time management. When you break down tasks into small, manageable chunks, you're less likely to feel overwhelmed. Instead of worrying about how much money you'll need to save to buy your dream home, figure out how much of each paycheque you'll need to put away. You'll feel much better.

Eliminate "I'm Busy" from Your Vocabulary

I'm tired of the "I'm busy" excuse. If I had a nickel for every time I heard someone say that, my mortgage would have been paid off a lot sooner. I hate to say it, but some of us aren't as busy as we say we are. You may be just choosing not to make certain things in your life a priority. Manage your time better to further your goal of burning your mortgage. When you manage your time better, you'll have time to earn extra money with side hustle (more on this in the appendix).

I live by a principle instilled in me by observing one of my idols, Mark Cuban, star of ABC's *Shark Tank* and the outspoken owner of the Dallas Mavericks. You've likely heard of return on investment, but have you ever heard of return on time? *Return on time* is the idea that you should value every minute of the day. Cuban is quoted as saying, "Work like there is someone working 24 hours a day to take it away from you." I live by this mantra.

On those days where there simply isn't enough time to get everything done, I figure out which tasks provide the greatest return on time. As a personal finance journalist, I'm often juggling deadlines, so it's important to prioritize and focus on those tasks that matter most.

Time management isn't important just in the workplace; it's important in everyday life. It's important to manage your time even for chores at home. For example, if you don't do the laundry, you might run out of clean clothes to wear, but if you don't mow the lawn, you can always do it tomorrow (unless it rains).

Like clockwork, each morning when I wake up, I write a to-do list. I write down everything I'd like to accomplish that day at both home and work. I find that once I set goals, it's relatively easy to manage my time. And I don't feel as stressed out by my workload. It helps me still find time to relax at the end of a long day.

If you're struggling with managing your time, try using a day planner and setting a schedule. Just as NFL coaches prepare for the next game, make a game plan for the day and coming week.

Stay Motivated

When it comes to your financials, unless you're a self-starter and enjoy reading personal finance books in your spare time (you must be the life of the party), it's helpful to have a financial planner or money coach on your side. These experts are like personal trainers for finances, setting realistic goals and breaking down those goals into manageable steps. They can help you draw up a financial plan to motivate you to make your financial dreams a reality. A financial plan looks at your current financial situation and then at where you'd like to be in the next five years and beyond. It sets your short- and long-term financial goals, and provides strategies on how you can achieve them. The cost of a financial plan may seem like a lot up front, but it's money well spent. Studies have found those with a written financial plan are more likely to achieve their financial goals. This includes owning a home.

So, how did I stay motivated to work long hours while paying off my mortgage? Even though I'm a very ambitious person and when I set a goal, I do everything in my power to achieve it, I'm the first to admit that putting in long hours can be tiring. Most mornings when the alarm sounded at 5 a.m., I felt like hitting the snooze button. But at least a couple of things kept me going.

Hiring a Superstar Financial Planner or Money Coach
Get referrals from family and friends. Interview a few to make sure they're a good fit. Ask for references from satisfied clients and follow up. Check their credentials to make sure they're qualified.

First, to help stay motivated, I framed newspaper articles about my goal of paying off my mortgage by age 31 and placed them on my desk. It didn't need to be newspaper articles—I might have framed an inspirational quotation or a photo. Whatever it is, as long as it motivates you, it can be the spark that keeps you going.

Second, I made myself accountable. The person you're accountable to acts as a motivator: you can tell each other about your goals and be a support system for one another. It might be your best friend, your brother or your mother—it doesn't matter. What matters is that you help keep each other motivated. Or you could simply hold yourself accountable to yourself... if you know that will work for you.

We all deal with setbacks from time to time, even highly successful people. Bill Gates was a Harvard University dropout and co-owner of a failed business called Traf-O-Data before he founded the world's largest software company, Microsoft. Whether it's losing your job or coming up short in a bidding war on your dream home, don't let it get you down. *Solutions for Financial Planning* offers this good advice: "Plan what you will do if you experience a setback, so that it doesn't stop you but becomes [only] a detour."[2] Learn from your mistakes on your way to achieving financial freedom.

Be sure to treat yourself once in a while. I'm not saying to go out and buy a 3D TV to celebrate a promotion at work, but you do need to have something to look forward to. Enjoy something you've been watching your spending on, like a meal at your favourite restaurant when you achieve a major milestone toward buying a home. It will motivate you that much more to work hard toward your next goal.

• • • • •

5 Key Mortgage-Burning Takeaways

➤ **Set goals.** Follow in the footsteps of successful people and set SMART goals. Put your SMART goals somewhere they will be a constant reminder of the promise of success you've made to yourself.

➤ **Work hard.** If homeownership were easy, everyone would own a home. Roll up your sleeves and be willing to work hard to make your dreams a reality.

➤ **Manage your time.** Try to eliminate "I'm busy" from your vocabulary. Do a better job of managing your time. Make financials goals such as paying off your mortgage a priority.

➤ **Draw up a financial plan.** A written financial plan helps motivate you to make your financial dreams a reality and keeps you accountable.

➤ **Stay motivated.** Setting a goal is only half the battle. Achieving it is the hardest part. Get family and friends to rally around you and keep you motivated.

A budget tells us what we can't afford,
but it doesn't keep us from buying it.
WILLIAM FEATHER, author

2

Budgeting and Tracking Your Spending
The Keys to Financial Freedom

FINANCIAL FREEDOM STARTS with understanding the basics of personal finance. You wouldn't want to run a marathon without training. Preparation is key for both.

In this chapter, you'll get a crash course on everything from building a budget and tracking your spending to giving your finances a checkup with a net worth statement. After reading this chapter, you'll be equipped with the tools and knowledge you need to take charge of your finances and achieve goals such as homeownership.

Budgeting and Tracking Spending

People work hard at school, at their job and at the gym, but when it comes to money, some of us don't show that same drive and determination. I get it—we live busy lives. The last thing you want to do at the end of a gruelling day is balance your chequebook. The thing is, until you get the fundamentals down pat, you won't be as successful as you could be.

Just because you earn a lot of money doesn't mean you'll have financial freedom. Just look at the NFL—the National Football League. Only two years after retirement, 78% of the players are bankrupt or financially stressed.[1] (No wonder they call it the "No Fun League"!) It's not about how much you *make*; it's how much you *save*.

A budget shows you how much money you have coming in and going out. It can help you break bad spending habits. Not having a budget is a lot like driving a car without a fuel gauge—you'll never know when you'll run out of fuel (read "money"). Unfortunately, many of us are driving in the dark. Surveys reveal that only about half of families have a budget.

Budgeting isn't just for middle-class families. In their book *The Millionaire Next Door*, authors Thomas Stanley and William Danko state that the majority of self-made million-aires have budgets. This should come as no surprise—a budget provides a big picture of your finances. You don't have to track your spending to the penny, but it is helpful to know where your money is going.

Most people know they should have a budget, so what's stopping them? The nega-tive stereotype of budgets has a lot to do with it. Yes, living within a budget can be boring, but it doesn't have to be. You can still have fun and enjoy your money; you just need to make smart decisions.

Budgeting can be an eye-opening expe-rience. Spending $2 here and there on pop and chocolate bars may not seem like a lot,

Budgeting for First-Time Homebuyers

A budget can be especially helpful for first-time home-buyers who are unaware of all the expenses that come with homeownership. Sit down with your parents or a friend who's a homeowner and pre-pare a budget for the home you'll own one day. Expenses to budget for include a mort-gage, utilities, property taxes and home insurance.

but discovering that you're spending $50 a month on these items may make you have second thoughts. By cutting back on discretion-ary spending, you can save more money toward the down payment on a home.

Living within a budget may not work for everyone, but at least cre-ating a budget is a good exercise to see exactly where you're spending your hard-earned money.

Find the way to budget that works for you—whether it's with a smartphone app or pen and paper. Stick to it and watch your finances improve.

Monthly Budgeting Made Easy

Here's a monthly budget you can use to track your spending. In the "estimate" column, write down how much you have budgeted for the month. At the end of the month, tally up your statements and receipts and write down the actual amount spent. You'll be able to see if your spending is in check or whether you're living beyond your means and need to cut back on non-essential items.

Ideally, you want a balanced budget. Any money left over can be allocated toward savings or debt repayment. That being said, since some expenses—electricity, gas and groceries, among others—are variable and can be higher than anticipated in any given month, aim for a slight surplus, maybe a net of $100, in case a surprise expense, like your washing machine breaking down, comes up.

Monthly Budget*

	$ Estimate (per month)	$ Actual (per month)	$ Difference
Income			
Income (after tax; best guess if necessary)			
Extra income (e.g., from side hustle [see the appendix], after tax; best guess if necessary)			
Rental income			
Total income (A)			
Expenses			
Mortgage and/or maintenance fees, or rent			
Electricity			
Gas			

* Visit SeanCooperWriter.com to download all worksheets from this book.

Water			
Property tax			
Home insurance			
Home maintenance and repairs			
Groceries			
Dental and medical			
Transportation (vehicle, transit, bike)			
Cable, Internet and phone			
Savings (down payment, emergency fund, etc.)			
Debt repayment (line of credit, credit card, loan, etc.)			
Support payments (spousal or child support)			
Clothing			
Entertainment (concerts, movies, music)			
Restaurants			
Gifts			
Travel			
Fitness			
Electronics (computers, smartphones, TVs)			
Personal care (haircuts, health and beauty products)			
Pets			
Other			
Total expenses (B)			
Net (A – B)			

Simple Ways to Track Spending

Preparing a budget is only half of the equation. It's just as important to track your spending on a monthly basis. Start by comparing your bills and receipts to the amounts noted in your budget to make sure you're not going over budget. Your budget isn't set in stone. Review it at least twice a year (or whenever there are major changes, like a raise at work or when you buy a home) to ensure it's up to date. Make changes as needed.

There are many tools out there to help you create a budget and track your spending. The Financial Consumer Agency of Canada has a helpful online budgeting calculator. Mint.com is also worth checking out—create a customized budget, manage your money and pay your bills from one convenient location. There's an abundance of budgeting apps for smartphones, such as Mint and Wally. If you're creating a family budget for the first time, try to keep it simple; you can create your own using a Microsoft Excel template.

Live Below Your Means

One of most basic rules of personal finance is to live *within* your means. I'd like to take that a step further and suggest that you live *below* your means. By living below your means, you'll achieve financial freedom sooner. You'll be able to prioritize your spending so you have enough money to cover the basics like mortgage, food and transportation and still have fun.

Measuring Your Personal Wealth: Net Worth

One of the easiest ways to measure your progress toward your financial goals is by tracking your net worth. Tracking your net worth is similar to an annual checkup at your doctor's. Not only does it show you how close you are to achieving your goals, it helps motivate you. Strive to grow your net worth long term. When your net worth grows, you'll be able to achieve long-term goals like saving toward the down payment on a home and paying off your mortgage.

Your net worth is similar to a business's balance sheet. You can calculate your net worth using this simple formula:

Net worth = Total assets – Total liabilities

   Total assets refers to everything you own, such as your home, investments and savings. *Total liabilities* are all the debts you owe, such as a car lease, student loan, credit card balance, line of credit or mortgage.

   There are many ways to track your net worth, including with apps. But I prefer using spreadsheet software, including Microsoft Excel. Google *net worth statement* for spreadsheet samples. GetSmarter-AboutMoney.ca has an excellent online net worth calculator. Tracking your net worth monthly is going overboard, so aim to track it on a quarterly basis, every three months.

Measuring Your Financial Health

Are your finances healthy? Complete this net worth statement to find out.

Net Worth Statement

As at (date)

Assets (what you own)

Cash and equivalent assets

Chequing accounts	$
Saving accounts	$

Investment assets

RRSPs	$
TFSAs	$
Non-registered investments (mutual funds, GICs, stocks, bonds)	$

Personal assets

Principal residence	$
Vehicles	$
Total assets (A)	$

Liabilities (what you owe)

Mortgage on principal residence	$
Credit card balance	$
Car loan/lease	$
Line of credit	$
Student loan	$
Total liabilities (B)	$
Total net worth (A – B)	$

Developing Good Money Habits

We all have money personalities. Some of us are savers, some of us are spenders and some of us fall somewhere in the middle. Many of us would like to save more money, but it's our behaviour that often gets in the way. Though we know we need to change our behaviour to get better results, that can be easier said than done.

As with bad eating habits, it's hard to break bad spending habits. If you haven't stepped foot inside a gym since high school, it's probably not realistic to plan to suddenly start going six days a week. If you aim to go only two or three times a week, your chances of success are much better. It's all about taking baby steps toward your goals. Many diets fail because they're too strict. It's hard to go from eating lunch at McDonald's every day to eating celery and carrots.

If you're spending more than you make, it's probably not realistic to set the goal of saving $1,000 a month. But by cutting back on your spending and setting a more realistic goal of, say, $200 or $300 a month, saving just got that much more manageable. You can eventually work your way up to $1,000 a month. By taking it slow, you're setting yourself up for success.

Small Purchases Can Add Up: The Latte Effect

Small daily purchases like Starbucks coffees and a McDonald's Big Mac combo may seem trivial, but overindulging in them can really add up. You may have heard of the *latte effect*. This refers to small, daily purchases that slowly empty your bank account. If you spend $5 a day on Starbucks coffee over 30 years, that adds up to almost $55,000. Think about how much money that is! You could save toward a down payment, pay down your mortgage sooner or retire early. And that's just one $5 latte.

I'm not saying to stop buying coffee at Starbucks (it's hard to beat a cold Frappuccino on a hot summer's day), but what I am saying is to carefully consider your spending decisions and how they'll affect your future self.

Keep an Eye on Recurring Bills
Monthly recurring bills like those for your cell phone, gym membership and cable can take a bite out of your budget. Look for ways to save. If you watch TV for only an hour a night, consider downgrading to basic cable or cancel cable altogether and go with Netflix.

Homeownership vs. Experience: How You Can Enjoy the Best of Both Worlds

Would you rather spend your money on stuff (e.g., homeownership) or experiences? For my generation, millennials, we're overwhelmingly choosing experiences. Seventy-eight percent would rather spend their money on an experience or event than purchase something desirable, like a home.[2] In fact, in the U.S., spending on live experiences and events compared to total consumer spending is up 70% since 1987. I suspect it's much the same scenario on this side of the border. Whether it's on a concert or a trip overseas, millennials would rather spend their money with their friends. Sixty-nine percent of millennials believe attending live experiences helps them connect better with their friends.

Millennials have been nicknamed the "renter generation," but most actually consider homeownership a key milestone in life. Eighty-six percent of Canadian millennials consider homeownership important—that's despite 42% of them renting and 21% living with their parents.[3]

Do you have to choose between homeownership and experience? Not necessarily. If your dream is to one day own a home, you may no longer be able to afford to stay at the nicest hotels in Europe or to dine at the finest restaurants, but maybe you can go backpacking instead (more on frugal travelling in chapter 4). Likewise, you may no longer be able to afford to join your friends for dinner every summer night on a patio, but maybe you can join them for drinks afterward instead. You just have to make your long-term financial goals like homeownership and financial freedom priorities.

Controlling Lifestyle Inflation While Still Having Fun

"Lifestyle inflation, what's that?" you may be asking. Before answering that question, let's look first at *inflation*—a sustained increase in prices, coupled with a decline in the purchasing power of money. For example, if the inflation rate is 3% annually, a chocolate bar that costs $1 today will cost $1.03 a year from now. Inflation may sound like a bad thing, but it's actually a sign of a healthy economy. A low level of inflation means consumers aren't spending, which is bad for the overall economy.

Lifestyle inflation is a term used to describe how our personal spending grows throughout our lives. So as you're promoted in your career, say, and your salary increases, typically so too does your spending. Why do we feel compelled to spend more? Often it's because of the people around us—we feel pressure to keep up with our family, friends, colleagues and neighbours. This may lead us to upsize our lifestyle by buying a new car, moving to a big house, going on expensive vacations and dining at fancy restaurants. It's one of the major factors leading to record-level household debt. Canadians owe $1.65 for every dollar of income earned.[4] The saying "Keeping up with the Joneses" has been replaced with "Keeping up with the Kardashians."

Although some lifestyle inflation is natural as our lives progress, if we're not careful, lifestyle inflation will wipe out any savings from that job promotion or new client contract.

Even if other people spend more on their lifestyle as they move up the corporate ladder, that doesn't mean *you* have to. I've avoided lifestyle inflation for the most part: when I was promoted from junior to senior pension analyst, I used my extra earnings to pay down my mortgage rather than saddling myself with bad debt.

So, what's the key to avoiding lifestyle inflation? Having a budget and making smart financially decisions. In these challenging economic times, ask yourself the tough questions: Do I really need a new car every three years? Aren't two televisions enough? Is an exotic vacation really necessary every year? Life is all about trade-offs.

The next time you get a promotion at work, by all means celebrate with a nice dinner out. Then consider putting a big chunk of your pay raise toward boosting your down payment or paying down your mortgage. It's okay to enjoy yourself, but try to set some money aside for long-term goals too.

Social Media and Overspending

Social media is ingrained in Western culture. Seventy-three percent of adults in Canada who are online use a social-networking site of some kind.[5] Many of us have a love-hate relationship with social media. It's great for connecting with friends, but many people admit that it makes them feel worse about their own lives. So not only is social media hurting our self-esteem, it's leading us to overspend.

Many millennials, for instance, have a YOLO (you only live once) attitude. Almost two-thirds (64%) of Canadian millennials surveyed admit to experiencing FOMO (fear of missing out).[6] That often means spending more because lower-priced products don't have the same social status as higher-end brands. Would you rather take a selfie in a pea coat from Club Monaco or in a winter coat from Walmart?

The same survey found that, in Canada, 56% of people between the ages of 18 and 30 feel driven to live beyond their means, and almost a quarter of young adults are concerned about losing their social status. FOMO is most often felt about travelling, parties and other events, and eating at high-end restaurants. The result? Big purchases for instant gratification—this while household debt is near a record high.

Whether you're a millennial, a Gen Xer or a baby boomer, it's possible to have a healthy life with social media. For starters, try not to compare yourself to others. Remember, you're only seeing snapshots of certain moments in people's lives. Ask yourself what you'd like to get out of social media. There are many ways to benefit from it—keeping in touch with friends and following the news, to name just a couple. But if you're feeling anxious, take a break. Spend a weekend away from your laptop, mobile phone and tablet, and reconnect with the world around you.

25 Ways to Save Big

We spend money on a lot of things in our daily lives. Spending $5 here and there may not seem like a lot, but by the end of the month, it can really add up. Not paying attention to how much you're spending can lead to living beyond your means. Here are some of the best ways to save money. I've included my best estimate of how much money you could be saving, along with strategic alternatives.

Everyday Spending

1 **Disposable products:** Not only do disposable products cost money, they hurt the environment. Instead of using plastic cutlery, use metal cutlery. Skip the paper napkins and go with reusable cloth napkins. Cloth dishrags are a good alternative to pricey paper towels. **Money you could save: $100 per year.**

2 **Lottery tickets:** You have a better chance of being struck by lightning than winning the lottery (no, I'm not making this up). Instead of spending $5 a week on a lottery ticket, consider putting that money toward your mortgage. **Money you could save: $260 per year.**

3 **Smartphone in-app purchases:** Most apps these days are free, but that doesn't mean you don't have to watch your spending here. The new trend is in-app purchases. If you're having trouble solving a crossword puzzle, the app may offer you a hint that you pay for. To avoid the temptation, turn off in-app purchases or add a passcode so you think twice before paying. **Money you could save: $520 per year.**

4 **Fuel:** Although the price at the pumps isn't as high as it once was, it still makes sense to plan out your driving trips ahead of time. GPS makes doing this a lot easier. Plan out your errands so you're not driving too far out of the way because you forgot to pick up milk and bread. Research driving techniques for fuel efficiency. **Money you could save: $500 per year.**

5 **Taxis and Uber:** Taking a taxi two or three blocks every day can really add up. When possible, take public transit, walk or cycle. If you take a taxi, try to split it with a group of friends. Uber (or a similar private-driver service) is a great way to save money—just watch out for its surge pricing: try to avoid using it during rush hour or in crowded places. **Money you could save: $1,000 per year.**

6 **Books, Blu-rays, digital movies and TV:** When's the last time you read a book or watched a movie more than once? Save yourself some money and use the public library (except for my book, of course; please ask your family and friends to buy it). Most libraries in big cities have an excellent selection of books, e-books, movies and TV shows. If you don't have cable, nothing beats Netflix. **Money you could save: $500 per year.**

7 **Deal websites:** Deal websites like Groupon are a great way to save money, as long as you don't become addicted. Avoid buying stuff you don't need by only visiting them when you plan to buy something. A further caution: only visit reputable websites. Avoid those with cheap copies of branded goods, expensive shipping costs to return items and short deadlines for refunds. **Money you could save: $500 per year.**

8 **Cigarettes:** For those of you who smoke, it's a costly habit. In 2015, the average price of a carton of 200 cigarettes was $88.64 in Ontario and $104.96 in B.C.[7] Butt out or cut back and save a bundle. **Money you could save: $2,000 per year.**

Recurring Monthly Expenses

9 **Gym memberships:** I'm all for people going to the gym and getting in shape, as long as they show up. But two-thirds of people with gym memberships never step foot inside a gym.[8] If you're joining a gym

for the first time, consider hiring a personal trainer for the first couple of weeks to show you the ropes. Once you get the hang of things, why not exercise with a buddy to keep each other motivated? If your condo has a decent gym, you can skip the gym membership fees altogether. **Money you could save: $700 per year.**

10 **Premium cable packages:** Do you really need 500-plus channels? Consider downgrading to basic cable or cut the cord altogether (more on this in chapter 5). Netflix and antennas are great cable alternatives. **Money you could save: $1,200 per year.**

11 **Utilities:** Do you sometimes forget to turn down the heat when you're leaving your home? In a typical home, about 60% of energy costs are from heating and cooling. Install a programmable thermostat, and in the wintertime set it so the temperature automatically goes up before you wake up, goes down when you leave home and then goes up again for when you arrive back home. Reduce the temperature by four to five degrees at night and when you're away to save 15% on your heating bill (but be mindful of any tenants; more on this in chapter 14). **Money you could save: $300 per year.**

Food and Alcohol

12 **Ready meals and prepared food:** If you're a foodie, it might be hard to imagine giving up your favourite dishes. You don't have to—you just have to be willing to find thrifty alternatives. Instead of picking up ready-made dishes like pasta, lasagna and side dishes at the supermarket and paying top dollar, consider taking cooking classes and learn to prepare them yourself, if you don't already know how. Weekdays can be hectic, so prepare your culinary masterpieces on weekends when you have more time. **Money you could save: $300 per year.**

13 **Bottled water:** Bottled water is marketing at its finest. You're paying for something that's available for free most places. Some argue that bottled water is higher quality than tap water, but usually it's no better. Save your money and stick to tap water and a Brita filter. Consider carrying a refillable water bottle with you on outings. **Money you could save: $300 per year.**

14 **Junk food:** Junk food in moderation might be fine. But if you're spending $20 a week on pop, chips and snacks, it's probably time to cut back. Shop with a grocery list to avoid impulse buys (more on this in chapter 5). **Money you could save: $1,040 per year.**

15 **Coffee:** Frequent visits to Starbucks can set you back some serious change. If you go to Starbucks twice a day every day, spending $10 on coffee each day, that's $70 per week, or $280 per month. Consider cutting back your visits to once a day and save $140 per month. Save yourself even more money and brew your own coffee. Carry it in a Thermos if you're travelling. **Money you could save: $1,825 per year.**

16 **Dining out:** Try to save dining out for celebrations, client meetings and special occasions. When possible, cook at home. Buying lunch on occasion is fine, but if you get into the habit of doing it every day, the spending can really add up. **Money you could save: $2,600 per year.**

17 **Alcohol:** There's nothing wrong with joining your colleagues for drinks on a Friday night, but buying a round of drinks every week can be costly. When possible, enjoy a pre-drink at home before going to a bar—that may be one less drink, at exorbitant bar prices, you'll pay for while out. **Money you could save: $780 per year.**

18 **Concession stands:** Tickets to concerts, movies and sporting events are expensive enough as they are. On top of that, we're expected to pay outrageous prices for food and drinks. At the Rogers Centre, home to the Toronto Blue Jays, you'll pay close to 10 bucks for a beer.[9] Save yourself some money by packing your own snack or dining out at an affordable restaurant beforehand. Although you can't bring your own beer into the venue, you'll save quite a bit by having that drink at home or limiting yourself to one drink during the game. **Money you could save: $300 per year.**

19 **Convenience stores:** We're all busy. But try to plan ahead, to avoid last-minute trips to the convenience store. Make a shopping list so you don't have to make a midnight run to 7-Eleven. **Money you could save: $500 per year.**

Big Purchases

20 Designer fashion: Why pay full price for a Prada handbag or Gucci shoes when you don't have to? Consignment and thrift stores are a great place to find brand-name fashion in good condition at discount prices. **Money you could save: $1,000 per year.**

21 Smartphones: We sure love our smartphones. Some of us would feel naked without them. But do you really need the latest iPhone when there's nothing wrong with your old one? Dropping $600-plus for a new iPhone every time a new version comes out gets pricey. Consider buying second-hand from a reputable retailer every couple of years and still enjoy the iPhone experience. **Money you could save: $1,000 per year.**

22 Rush delivery: Unless you need something immediately (maybe you forget your wedding anniversary), plan ahead and go with regular shipping. Rush delivery can cost almost as much as the product itself. **Money you could save: $100 per year.**

Banking and Credit Cards

23 Credit card interest: Follow the golden rule of using credit cards wisely and spend only what you can afford to pay off in full once your credit card balance comes due, and you will never pay interest. Unfortunately, not everyone follows this simple principle (more on credit cards in chapter 3). **Money you could save: $1,000 per year.**

24 Bank fees: Many of us are paying bank fees when we don't have to. Switch to low- and no-fee banking and save your money (more on bank fees in chapter 3). **Money you could save: $240 per year.**

25 Payday loans: Each year, millions of people pay triple-digit interest rates for these short-term loans. (Interestingly, Facebook and Google have banned payday loan ads from their sites.) Do yourself a favour and avoid them like the plague. Have a rainy-day fund for surprise expenses (more on emergency funds in chapter 13). **Money you could save: $520 per year.**

Total money you could save: $19,085 per year.

Still think spending $2 here and there isn't a big deal? By being a smart shopper, you can save a bundle and be that much closer to buying a home and paying it off.

How Much Money Could You Be Saving?

How much money could you be saving by being a little more thrifty? Complete this table to find out.[10] I've started you off with a couple of examples. From the list of items or services above, determine where your spending is out of whack and come up with alternatives of your own. Then total up how much money you could be saving.

Item or service	Monthly cost	Alternative	New monthly cost	Monthly savings
Bought lunch	$300	Packed lunch	$50	$250
Cable TV	$150	Netflix	$10	$140
Total				

• • • • •

5 Key Mortgage-Burning Takeaways

➤ **Create a budget**. To avoid impulse purchases and overspending, create a budget and track your spending. Any extra money you find you can put toward your down payment or mortgage.

➤ **Prepare a net worth statement.** A net worth statement measures your progress toward your goals. It also will help motivate you and keep you accountable.

➤ **Watch your daily spending.** Small daily purchases like Starbucks coffees may seem trivial but can really add up. Consider cutting back from two such purchases a day to one.

➤ **Curb lifestyle inflation.** Try to stop comparing yourself against others. When you get a pay raise, bank most of it. Unplug from social media every now and then.

➤ **Look for ways to save.** Review your budget and find ways to save. For example, just by cutting back on bottled water, you could save about $300 a year.

Life was a lot simpler when what we honored was
father and mother rather than all major credit cards.
ROBERT ORBEN, professional comedy writer

3

Credit Cards and Banking
Use (Don't Abuse)
These Financial Tools

NOW THAT YOU'VE mastered the basics of personal finance, it's time to tackle the topic of credit cards and banking. The first credit card in widespread use in the 1950s was the Diners Club card. It was known as a "charge" card because the balance was to be paid in full each month. Not too long afterward, revolving balance was introduced. This let you carry a balance on your card. Slowing but surely, cardholders started carrying balances on their credit cards (as they were now known), until it was a regular thing. And in Canada, credit card usage has been steadily climbing for years. In fact, we're seeing a shift to a cashless society: Seventy-one percent of Canadians surveyed say they're comfortable never handling cash again.[1]

In this chapter, you'll learn the basics of credit cards and banking, and how to get the most out of your credit card. Are you paying banking fees? With low-fee and no-fee banking, chances are you don't have to be. I'll show you how to choose the bank account that will meet all your daily financial needs.

Credit Cards: Powerful Financial Tools

Credit cards are a powerful financial tool when used responsibly. They can be used to build your credit score, manage your short-term cash flow and earn rewards points or other promotions. It's when you start carrying a balance that you run into trouble. Think about these credit card fast facts:

- Canadians made over 11.5 billion cashless transactions in 2014— 3.9 billion of those transactions were with a credit card; 4.9 billion, a debit card.[2]
- In 2014, 72 million Visa and MasterCard credit cards were in circulation in Canada.[3] That's more than two credit cards for every Canadian.
- Canadians carried an average credit card debt of $3,745 in 2015.[4]
- Nearly half (46%) of Canadians carry a balance on their credit card.[5]

I could rant about why we shouldn't carry a balance on our credit cards, but that would be pointless. Half of Canadians *already* carry a balance. Credit card debt is as much a part of Canadian culture as hockey and maple syrup. If you find yourself in this situation and you're tired of paying sky-high interest charges (typically 19%), there's a way out. It all comes down to getting out of debt and living below your means.

Your Credit Card Is *Not* an Emergency Fund

A credit card is not a rainy-day fund. It's generally recommended that you have three to six months' living expenses set aside in a savings account in case you find yourself in a financial pickle. My friend Sarah recently found herself in this very situation. Sarah was between jobs for three months. During this time she racked up $2,000 in credit card debt. Only paying the minimum payment, she was barely putting a dent in the interest. It would take her over 10 years and cost her thousands of dollars in interest to pay off. If she had a rainy-day fund, she could have drawn on it instead of using her credit card for cash advances and certain purchases, and avoided paying the exorbitant credit card interest rates.

Four Simple Ways to Control Your Credit Card Spending

It's easier than ever to pay for goods and services with your credit card. Simply tap or swipe it and spend $50 in the blink of an eye. Although credit cards offer a convenient way to spend, that convenience comes at a cost. Not only can credit cards cost you a bundle in interest, but we tend to spend more when we make purchases with a credit card instead of cash—12% to 18% more.[6]

The pain you feel upon seeing the steep price of a Rolex watch is caused by stimulation in a part of your brain known as the insula. But when you use your credit card, the pain is dulled (since you're not handing over actual money). Even if you're careful, credit cards can turn you into a big spender. If you're buying a pair of Nike sneakers, what's more painful, swiping your credit card or handing over $20 bills? I'm willing to bet it's the latter.

So, how do you control your credit card spending? Here are four simple ways:

1 **Leave your credit card at home.** Carry your credit card only when you plan to make purchases. If your credit card is sitting at home in your dresser drawer, you'll be forced to pay with cash or debit and might think twice about frivolous purchases like a new blazer (especially when your closet is already jam-packed with a dozen of them).

2 **Take a cooling-off period.** Before you swipe your credit card for a major purchase, give yourself a cooling-off period. Unless the sale is ending that day or there's only one left in your size, you can always go back another day. Take the time to think in the comfort of your home.

3 **Avoid spending triggers.** Do you ever head to the mall just to window shop, only to come out with a shopping bag full of stuff? Try not to go to the mall unless you actually need something. Go for a walk to the gym, the park or the library instead.

4 **Switch to cash only.** If you've tried all of the above but still can't keep your spending under control, it might be time for something more drastic. Deal in cash only until you can get your spending under control.

EXAMPLE CREDIT CARD INTEREST CAN BE COSTLY

Mary-Kate Olsen goes on a shopping spree in Manhattan (Ashley decides to stay home because she's still bummed out about being excluded from *Fuller House.*) Mary-Kate ends up charging $3,000 on her credit card for a new wardrobe. She doesn't have any big acting gigs lined up, and all her money is tied up in her fashion empire, but she thinks, *What's the harm? I'll carry a balance on my credit card.* When she gets her credit card statement, Mary-Kate has two choices: she can pay the minimum payment of $90 (the greater of 3% or $10) or she can pay a higher amount. We'll assume she pays an interest rate of 18% on her credit card. Let's look at both scenarios.

	Option A: Minimum payment	Option B: Higher payment
Payment amount	$90	$250
Time to being debt-free	16 years	1 year, 2 months
Original balance	$3,000	$3,000
Total interest	$2,798.88	$332.67
Total paid (principal and interest)	$5,798.88	$3,332.67
Interest saved	–	$2,466.21
Time saved	–	14 years, 10 months

If Mary-Kate pays the minimum of $90 (this amount decreases as she pays off her balance), not only will it take her almost 15 years to pay off her credit card but her wardrobe will end up costing her nearly double what she initially paid for it ($5,798.88) once interest is included. But if Mary-Kate decides to pay a higher amount, $250 per month, she'll pay her credit card debt in a little over one year and save $2,466.21 in interest. Not bad! The moral of the story: Pay off your credit card as fast as you can, before interest piles on. Better yet, avoid impulse buys and carrying a balance in the first place (even if you only owe $1 on an original balance of $4,000, you'll be charged interest on the entire amount from the date you made the purchase until it's fully repaid—*ouch!*).

If you're curious to see how much your credit card interest is costing you, check out the Financial Consumer Agency of Canada's credit card payment calculator.

Eight Do's and Don'ts for Credit Cards

Looking to get your credit card spending under control? Here are some simple do's and don'ts. Tear out this page and post it on the ceiling above your bed (just don't blame me for damaging your book). Or better yet, photocopy it.

1 **Do** purchase only what you can afford to pay off in full once your statement comes due.

2 **Do** read the fine print. Make sure you know everything there is to know about your credit cards, from fees for missing a payment to the length of your interest-free grace periods.

3 **Do** check your statement weekly. This may seem excessive, but keeping an eye on your spending is a good way to keep it in check.

4 **Don't** carry a balance on your credit card.

5 **Don't** sign up for too many credit cards. It can tempt you to overspend and lower your credit score.

6 **Don't** do cash advances. Not only are you dinged with fees, the interest rate can be upward of 30%.

7 **Don't** use your credit card as an emergency fund. Have three to six months' living expenses readily available in your savings account for a rainy day.

8 **Don't** make purchases just to earn reward points. Spending to earn 1% rewards while paying 18% interest just doesn't make sense.

Get Out of Credit Card Debt

If you want to own a home, make getting out of debt your top priority. Because of the high interest rates of credit cards, your credit card balance can grow quickly. Too much debt can mean qualifying only for a low mortgage amount—or not qualifying at all. Debt can also put a strain on your relationship. When polled, 68% of couples said fighting over money would be their top reason for divorce, followed by infidelity (60%).[7]

There are two popular ways to pay down debt: *debt avalanche* and *debt snowball*. With debt avalanche, you pay down the debt with the *highest interest rate*, whereas with debt snowball, you pay down the debt in order *from smallest to largest balance*. There's no one right way. Choose the method that works for you, continue paying at least the minimum monthly payment to keep your credit in good standing, and do what it takes to get the heck out of debt!

EXAMPLE PAYING DOWN CREDIT CARD DEBT

Lily's two credit cards both have outstanding balances. To pay down her debt sooner, she works part time on the weekends as a bank teller, earning an extra $500 a month. Using *debt avalanche*, she could pay $410 per month toward her retail credit card (which has the higher interest rate of her two cards) while paying the minimum, $90 per month, on her MasterCard. By using *debt snowball*, she could pay $350 per month toward her MasterCard (which has the smallest balance) while paying the minimum, $150 per month, on her retail credit card:

	MasterCard	Retail Credit Card
Balance	$3,000	$5,000
Interest rate	19%	28%
Minimum monthly payment	$90	$150

Lily will save the most in interest by paying off her retail credit card first, but she might find paying off her MasterCard more motivating, since it has the smallest balance and she'd pay it off sooner.

Mobile Payments: The Cost of Convenience

It's getting harder and harder to keep our spending in check. And the rise in popularity of mobile payments isn't making it any easier. Heading to the mall with a wallet full of credit cards could soon be a thing of the past. With Canada's big banks partnering with Apple Pay, mobile payment seems to be the way of the future. You can now order a Starbucks coffee ahead of time to avoid the lineup.

Although mobile payment is a convenient and fast way to make everyday purchases, it comes with a major risk: overspending. We're even more likely to overspend with our mobile phone than with credit cards (some people are so addicted to their smartphone, you couldn't pry it out of their hands).

Since you're limited to purchases of under $100 with Apple Pay, major purchases are not a big concern, but impulse purchases are. Before entering your PIN to buy something, take a timeout and ask yourself, do I really need this? If you're unsure, wait 24 hours. Chances are the answer will be no.

Choosing a Low-Fee or No-Fee Bank Account

Keep Your Mobile Spending in Check

If you decide to use a digital wallet like Apple Pay, download a budgeting app (Mint is one) to track your spending. You'll be less likely to overspend the next time you see a sale at H&M.

Recently I was surprised to learn how much my friend Matthew was paying in bank fees. The bank was charging him $15 a month just for having a chequing account. Far too many of us are paying bank fees when we don't need to. Almost half (46%) of customers of Canada's big five banks said they pay monthly fees.[8] Yet many people aren't willing to go through the effort of switching to low-fee or no-fee banking. Hopefully I can change your mind.

Let's say you're paying $15 a month for your chequing account. If you pay $15 a month for the next 25 years (the length of most mortgages), you'll end up spending $4,500 in bank fees (that's assuming fees don't go up, which they almost certainly will).

Ask yourself this, what benefit are you getting from paying bank fees? Is the friendly chat with the teller and "free" cup of coffee really worth $4,500?* There are online tools, like Tangerine's Switch Assistant, that make switching banks a breeze. Instead of paying bank fees, why not put that money toward your down payment or closing costs?

Nine Things to Look for in a Bank Account

Curious how your bank account stacks up against the competition? Here are nine things to look for to make your banking experience a pleasant one:

---

* I'm not saying it never makes sense to get a bank account with a big bank. If you're able to avoid paying bank fees by maintaining a monthly balance and enjoy perks like free e-transfers, it may be worth it.

1 **Excellent customer service:** Customer service is at the top of the list. Look for a bank with a reputation for excellent customer service. There's nothing more annoying than spending your precious time on the phone, on hold.

2 **Low- or no-fee:** There are plenty of banking options out there with no monthly fees—Tangerine and PC Financial are just two. You can't escape fees altogether. Low-fee and no-fee banks typically charge fees for everything from bounced cheques to money transfers. Ask ahead of time about the fees for the services you'll use and choose a bank whose fees are low.

3 **Low or no minimum balance:** At many banks, a minimum balance is necessary in order to avoid bank fees. I don't have a problem with a $500 minimum balance, but some banks require a minimum balance of $2,000 or higher. Drop below your minimum balance at any point in the month and you're dinged with fees.

4 **Unlimited transactions:** Some banks impose limits on how many free transactions and teller visits you can have a month. Avoid this headache altogether and go with a bank that offers unlimited transactions.

5 **Large ATM network:** There's nothing more annoying than not being able to find an ATM when you need it. With many banks offering cheque deposit via mobile phone, this isn't as important as it once was, but it can still be handy to have an ATM nearby, especially if you want to withdraw cash.

6 **Online and mobile banking:** A user-friendly and secure website and mobile app are crucial. You'll want to be able to conveniently withdraw, deposit and transfer money.

7 **Deposit insurance:** Make sure your bank is covered by the Canada Deposit Insurance Corporation, which protects your money if the bank goes bankrupt. Credit unions have provincial deposit insurance.

8 **Decent interest rate:** Low- and no-fee banks tend to offer higher interest rates for savings accounts than the big banks since their overhead costs are lower. Be sure to shop around.

9 **Dedicated savings account:** Dedicated savings accounts are a nice-to-have. They let you separate your funds for different purposes. For example, if you're saving toward a down payment, you'll want to keep that money separate from your emergency fund.

Three Easy Ways to Save on Bank Fees

1 Keep a minimum monthly balance. Keep your account balance above the minimum balance to avoid being dinged by bank fees.
2 Limit your visits to bank tellers. Most banks put a limit on the number of bank teller visits you have before being charged a fee for their services. Use ATMs, online or mobile banking instead.
3 Avoid other banks' ATMs. Plan ahead to avoid spur-the-moment cash withdrawals from other banks' ATMs (the fees are sky-high). Or ask for cash back when you use your debit card.

• • • • •

5 Key Mortgage-Burning Takeaways

➤ **Use your credit card responsibly.** Only buy what you can afford to pay off in full once your credit card statement comes due.

➤ **Avoid spending triggers.** If every time you go to the mall, you end up buying something, only go to the mall when you absolutely need to make a purchase.

➤ **Get out of debt.** Two popular ways to pay down debt are debt avalanche and debt snowball. Make a debt-free plan and stick to it. It's easier to qualify for a mortgage when you're debt-free.

➤ **Avoid bank fees.** Bank fees really add up over time. Consider switching to a bank that offers low- or no-fee banking and save a bundle.

➤ **Save for your down payment.** Look for a bank that offers dedicated savings accounts. These accounts let you sock away your money for different goals, like saving toward your down payment.

Beware of little expenses.
A small leak will sink a great ship.
BENJAMIN FRANKLIN

4

Getting the Biggest Bang for Your Buck
"Frugal" Is Not a Four-Letter Word

I'M GOING TO begin this chapter by talking about the f-word: *frugality*. Frugality—which started way back when with coupon clipping—has gone mainstream. Being frugal is the new "in" thing. A few years ago, if someone had called me frugal, I'd think they were calling me cheap, but today I'd take it as a compliment. Instead of doing the Canadian thing and apologize for my frugal ways, I'm embracing my thriftiness.

Frugality isn't just about saving money. It's about getting the biggest bang for your buck. Being frugal pays off—it's the key to reaching mortgage freedom.

Just like the TV series *MythBusters*, I'm going bust a myth right now: you can be frugal and still enjoy your money. You don't have to give up your favourite things in life. You just have to be smart with your spending.

46

Live Frugally, Not Like a Cheapskate

Being frugal isn't the same as being cheap. When you're cheap, you always choose the lowest-priced option, ignoring quality. When you're frugal, you choose the product or service that offers the best value for your money. Not only can being a cheapskate cost you more money in the end, it can cost you your friends. Here are four things you shouldn't cheap out on:

- **Home renovations:** Hiring the contractor with the lowest quote can set you up for disaster. If you're doing major home renovations, get in writing quotes from at least three contractors. If a quote is a lot lower than the others, it may be a warning sign that the contractor is cutting corners to save you money. Often it's best to choose a quote that's somewhere in the middle (more about hiring a contractor in chapter 9).

- **Gifts:** No one wants to show up at a social gathering empty-handed. If you're on a tight budget, come up with something creative. For example, a friend of mine once drew portraits for her friends. This meant a lot more to them than just another gift card.

- **Clothing:** Investing in your appearance is money well spent. In the business world, you want to "dress for success," to stand out from the competition. That being said, you don't have to spend a mint and show up at your company's holiday party in an Armani suit. Be a smart shopper and take the time to comparison shop. Buy clothes when they're on sale.

- **Electronics:** These are expensive enough as it is. Buying the cheapest option can come back to haunt you if it's unreliable and continually breaks down. Before you buy, do your homework by reading customer reviews and comparing features. Think twice about purchasing refurbished products (some have already broken down once).

Four Simple Ways to Save Money While Shopping

Do you ever find yourself coming out of the mall spending more than you planned to? Retailers use every trick in the book to make us spend more—upsizing shopping baskets and tempting us to make impulse buys such as chocolate bars and magazines at the point of purchase. It's time to fight back! Live by these four simple rules to keep more money in your wallet next time you head to the mall.

1. Stick Up for Your Money

A lot of people are shy to ask for a deal. Don't be. Whether you're asking for a discount on a pair of shoes or on a car, stick up for your money. I'm going to share nine magic words with you that will change your life: *Is this the best price you can offer me?* If you don't ask for a discount, you won't get one. I recently saved $20 on a pair of boots on clearance just by asking this simple question.

When you're asking for a discount, be polite yet persistent. To avoid holding up the line, ask a salesperson before heading to the cashier. If you're not getting anywhere, politely ask to speak to a manager. It doesn't hurt to mention you've been a loyal customer for years. You may not think it's worth the hassle, but saving $10 here and there really adds up.

Shop with Your Smartphone and Save

Comparison shopping is now easier than ever thanks to smartphone apps, such as RedFlag-Deals and Wish. Find out about the best deals in an instant.

2. Comparison Shop

You may be getting a good deal, but how will you know for sure if you don't see what else is out there? Take the time to comparison shop. If you're looking for a new coat or pair of shoes, check the flyers of other stores to see if you can find a better deal.

If you're simply looking for an item in general, like new shoes, and not a specific brand, before you decide to buy, visit at least three stores. You might find nicer shoes at a lower price (you'll never know if you just go with the first shoes you come across).

3. Never Pay Full Price

Plan ahead to avoid paying full price for anything. Retail competition is fierce, so use that to your advantage. Before going shopping, browse the flyers for items you need. Many retailers are willing to price match.

Showing some spending restraint can pay big dividends. For example, if you buy a new coat today, it might cost you $600, but if you wait four weeks, say, until it's "out of season," that same coat may cost only $300, or less. For items from clothing to electronics and everything in between, I've almost never paid full price for anything, and you shouldn't either.

Dealing with Peer Pressure

Why do we overspend? It has a lot to do with the company we keep. Peer pressure affects who we are and the actions we take. If you hang out with friends who like to overspend, guess what? You're more likely to overspend too.

Let's say your colleagues go out for coffee. Instead of joining them every day, perhaps only go once or twice a week. You'll save money and still be able to bond. Going to restaurants is another easy way to spend a lot, and you don't want to only drink tap water and eat bread. Still join your friends, but instead of ordering a full course, consider ordering just an appetizer or salad, or meet up afterward for drinks.

---

4. Pay Attention at the Checkout

Paying attention at the checkout can save you money. Each year, U.S. consumers lose between $1 billion and $2.5 billion because of scanner errors.[1] Undoubtedly, Canadian consumers too are losing a lot of money at the checkout. When I worked at a supermarket, I lost count of how many times scanner errors occurred. As a consumer, you typically make the decision to purchase a product based on its price tag. An item scanning at a higher price may be one you no longer wish to purchase. Pay attention to price tags when cruising the store aisles. When you get to the checkout, watch how much the items scan at. It can be hectic at the checkout, so be sure to review your receipt before leaving the store.

If you're overcharged for an item, politely but firmly speak up for your money. At stores that abide by the national Scanner Price Accuracy Voluntary Code (and with a few exceptions), you're entitled to the item for free if it's under $10, or to $10 off the item if it's over $10.

Although the code is voluntary, almost every major retailer in Canada has adopted it. Don't be afraid to mention the code; some retailers won't offer you the item for free or discounted unless asked to. For more information, visit the Retail Council of Canada website.

Love, Money and Relationships

I've never been married, and I've never planned a wedding, but I do know that relationships offer a lot of benefits, both emotional and financial. Relationships make homeownership a lot easier when it comes to qualifying for a mortgage (assuming there are two salaries instead of just one), but they don't come cheap. Have you ever wondered how much a relationship costs? RateSupermarket.ca took the time to crunch the numbers and put a price tag on love.

From the first date to walking down the aisle, couples spend on average a heart-stopping $61,822, according to the 2016 Cost of Love study.[2] To put this into perspective, unmarried couples spend more on relationships than the average down payment of a first-time homebuyer. (The average first-time homebuyer in Canada expects to put down $48,000 on a $300,000 home.)[3] Not only that, but the cost of love is rising a lot faster than inflation—it's up 22.8% year over year.

In the dating phase, couples spend an average of $10,684 per year. The most costly expenses include fancy dates (each at an average of $278), weekend getaways ($626), beach vacations ($1,762) and the man's wardrobe ($1,347).

It doesn't get any less expensive when you get engaged. A couple's average cost for a one-year engagement is $12,165. That includes another year of dating and a wardrobe update ($5,178), an engagement ring ($4,987) and an engagement party ($2,000).

If you think that's expensive, you ain't seen nothing yet. The average cost of tying the knot is $38,973. Some of the most costly expenses include clothing for the bride ($2,105) and groom ($637), the ceremony ($2,875), the reception ($15,227) and the honeymoon ($2,424).

I'm not saying you shouldn't get married—that's crazy talk. But what I am saying is to watch your budget. For many people, their wedding day is the most important day of their lives, and that's fine. By overspending on your wedding, you may have to push back realizing your dream of homeownership by a few years.

Making the Most of Your Wedding Expenses

You'll likely be spending a lot when you walk down the aisle. You can still have a dream wedding without a boatload of debt. Make the most of your wedding expenses with these practical tips:

- Charge everything on your credit card to earn rewards points or cash back. RateSupermarket.ca has a handy tool to help you select the best card based on your spending. (Just make sure you can pay off those expenses in full once your balance comes due; otherwise, you'll face hefty interest charges.)

- If you and your partner are first-time homebuyers, consider putting cash gifts toward your down payment (provided you have any money left over after the wedding and "moneymoon").

- Don't start married life in debt. As soon as you get engaged, start a dedicated savings account for your engagement and wedding expenses. If you decide to go into debt to finance your wedding, choose lower-interest options like a line of credit over credit cards.

- The traditional rule of thumb when buying a fiancée's engagement ring is to spend two to three months' salary. That's a lot of money! Consider buying the ring at a pawn shop or estate jewellery shop, and have it polished or cleaned (just don't blame me if your bride calls off the engagement).

- With reality TV shows like *Say Yes to the Dress*, it's no surprise brides have spent a lot of money by the time they walk the aisle. To save on your wedding dress, check out trunk shows or consider renting.

- If homeownership is a priority, take a honeymoon at a local destination. You can always have your dream honeymoon later on, once you've bought a home and you're well on the way to paying off your mortgage.

Travelling for Less

Travelling is many things to many people. When I was paying off my mortgage, I didn't go on extravagant trips, but that doesn't mean you have to be like me. It's all about setting financial priorities. Now that my mortgage is paid off, I can travel as much as I want.

The average Canadian spends $1,800 per trip.[4] If you can't afford to travel right now, you can always take a staycation. If you live in a big city like Calgary, Toronto or Vancouver, there are plenty of events and festivals in the summer to enjoy.

If you're planning a big trip, save up ahead of time and try not to go into debt for it. If you're planning to go on a trip to Paris next summer, say, figure out how much you need to save. If the trip costs $2,000 and there are 10 months until your trip, you'll need to save $200 a month. Set up a dedicated savings account for travel and deposit the money via direct deposit or preauthorized transfers from each paycheque.

Save on Food While Travelling

To save on costly eating out, share plates and use Yelp to find restaurants with good ratings and reasonable prices. Typically, dishes are less expensive at lunchtime than at dinnertime. Food markets are great places to pick up prepared food or sandwich ingredients for a picnic in the park or at the beach. Cold cereal is a simple breakfast that's easy to prepare and eat in a hotel room. Or choose a hotel with complementary continental breakfast.

There are plenty of ways to save on travel. Book your flight, hotel or car rental through online travel companies such as Expedia, PC Travel and Travelocity, or redeem your credit card travel reward points toward your flight. Hotels can be expensive (especially in the downtown core), so consider staying at hostels or joining the sharing economy and using Airbnb or similar online rental service (just make sure you get a contract and review it thoroughly). Flying the whole family can be costly, so consider driving instead. If you decide to take a road trip, have your car serviced before leaving, to avoid being stranded on the side of the road, and plan out your route to avoid tolls.

If you're travelling outside Canada, to save on currency exchange, sign up for a credit card like Amazon.ca Rewards Visa Card or Rogers

Platinum MasterCard, which have no foreign exchange fees. For pocket change, you're usually better off exchanging money at home at your bank before leaving for your trip rather than at currency booths in airports and train stations, which typically offer the worst rates.

You don't have to spend a bundle to have fun—look for free activities like festivals and bundles online. See the top tourist attractions in North America at a discount with CityPASS.

• • • • •

5 Key Mortgage-Burning Takeaways

➤ **Be frugal, not cheap.** Being frugal is about getting the biggest bang for your buck; being cheap is spending the least amount of money, period. Being cheap can cost you more in the long run.

➤ **Comparison shop.** You may be getting a good deal, but how will you know for sure? Use smartphone apps to check out prices at other stores.

➤ **Pay attention at the checkout.** Watch to see how much the item scans for. If you're overcharged, don't be afraid to speak up for your money.

➤ **Don't blow your wedding budget.** Try not to start married life in debt. Look for ways to save and still have your dream wedding. It could mean the difference between buying your dream home today and moving in with the in-laws.

➤ **Travel for less.** Save up for travelling and don't go into debt for it. Save money by booking your flight through an online travel company and your accommodations with an online rental services.

The way to build your savings is by
spending less each month.
SUZE ORMAN, financial adviser and TV host

5

Food, Home
Entertainment and Phones
Saving on the Things You Love

AFTER SHELTER (mortgage or rent), the two most costly expenses for most families are food and transportation (more about transportation in chapter 6). If you want to own a home and pay it off sooner, you're going to have to be smart with big purchases. These two spending categories are a great place to start.

When I was paying off my mortgage, I kept my food expenses to a minimum (it helped that I'm vegetarian) and still ate healthy. With the money I saved, I made lump-sum payments on my mortgage, saving thousands of dollars in interest. You may not want to cut back on your grocery budget as much as I did, but there are still simple and easy ways to reduce your grocery bill.

In the first half of the chapter we'll concentrate on saving on food. Of course, you'll still want to have fun while you're paying off your mortgage, so in the second half, we'll look at saving on home entertainment and cell phones.

Save More on Groceries

Do you find it challenging to keep your grocery spending on budget? You're not alone. For most of us, groceries are the second-highest expense after putting a roof over our heads. With temptation down every aisle, it's not hard for your grocery spending to spiral out of control. And it's getting more and more expensive to feed a family. Food prices at the supermarket are rising a lot faster than the rate of inflation. Not only are prices going up, but product packaging is getting smaller, in what's known as *downsizing*. Instead of raising prices, food companies pass cost increases on to you by reducing package sizes. Everything from bags of bread to jars of pasta sauce are getting smaller—a jar that was once 700 millilitres is now only 650 millilitres. We're being asked to pay more for less.

You don't need to give up your favourite foods to pay down your mortgage sooner. You just need to know how to stretch your grocery dollars further.

Shop at Discount Supermarkets

How would you like to buy your staples for a lot less? Have you considered shopping at discount supermarkets? At premium stores, you'll spend a dollar or more extra on everything from breakfast cereal to coffee. The savings at discount supermarkets can really add up. By buying no-name brands you can save even more—typically 25% less than the price of premium brands. Shaving $20 off your grocery bill each week will add up to savings of over $1,000 a year.

Discounts grocers often have produce and meat that is just as good quality as the so-called premium stores. You don't have to stop shopping at your local grocer altogether; rather, consider your other options.

Throw Out Less Food and Save

Each year, the average household throws out hundreds of dollar worth of food.[1] Throw out less food by watching expiry dates and keeping your fridge and cupboards organized.

Make a Shopping List and Price Match

To avoid overspending, make a shopping list and browse the flyers, either those delivered to your door or online. Look for deals on products you plan to buy. Apps like Flipp, which let you check out weekly flyers from the convenience of your smartphone, make saving money easier.

Why pay full price for groceries when you don't have to? You can save even more money by price matching, whereby retailers match a competitor's lower price on identical items if you point it out to them (you'll need to show the competitor's flayer as proof). Many discount supermarkets price match. Price matching is a weekly ritual for me. Each week before going grocery shopping I make a shopping list. I go through my fridge, freezer and cupboards to see what items I'm running low on. Once armed with my list, I'll look for these products in store flyers.

Through price matching, especially big savings are to be had on household items like toilet paper and laundry detergent, which are typically pricey. Instead of wasting time and energy visiting various supermarkets, I'm able to purchase almost everything at one store. It doesn't get any easier than that!

Buy Items on Sale and in Bulk

When you see a grocery item on sale, take advantage of it and stock up. But before loading your cart full of jars of spaghetti sauce, remember that not all sales are created equal. See how much money you're actually saving to determine whether it's worth stocking up. Plus, some items that appear in the flyer might be listed at regular, not sale, price, so don't be fooled. Any given item typically goes on sale at a particular store every two to three months, so stock up accordingly.

Save on Meat

No, that's not your steak being grilled, it's your wallet. Sizzling meat prices can really take a bite out of your grocery budget. I'm not saying you have to give up striploin steaks and pork chops, but by cutting back on meat, you'll save money and eat healthier. You might choose to eat meat less often, or buy cuts that are on sale (cheaper cuts may be tougher but will become tender if slow cooked).

Buy in Season

Buying your favourite fruits and vegetables out of season will cost you. Have you seen the price of cherries in January? Yikes! Consider holding out on your favourite fruits and vegetables until they're in season, and buying produce that *is* in season. So instead of buying watermelons during the winter, purchase less costly fruits, like apples and oranges. If you're not ready to give up your favourite fruit, you can still save money by buying it less frequently—only twice a month instead of every week, say. This way, it will be more of a treat too.

Save on Electricity

Save money on your electricity bill by using a microwave or toaster oven to warm up food, rather than heating the entire range oven. Save even more by turning off devices when not in use—having several plugged into a power bar makes turning them all off easier.

Make Your Meals

Instead of buying TV dinners or fast food, make your own meals. I know it can be tempting to pick up fast food on the way home after a long day at the office. We all do this every once in a while. But if you limit dining out to only once or twice a week, the savings can really add up. By cooking at home, you'll save money and eat healthier too.

And how about cooking your meals in batches? I often work up to 80 hours per week—and if I can manage to cook my own meals, so can you. What's my secret? I prepare them in advance. Over the weekend I batch cook several meals, freezing them for the upcoming week. When I get home from a long day at the office, all I do is warm up my meal in the microwave or oven and it's ready to eat in under five minutes. (For variety, I rotate through the meals in the freezer.) It doesn't get any easier than that.

Save on Home Entertainment

Are you tired of shelling out thousands of dollars to the cable company each year for hundreds of channels you don't watch? Why not join the growing trend and ditch cable TV? One in six Canadians doesn't have cable and instead streams TV shows and movies online.[2] Ditching cable and living cable-free is commonplace these days—"cord cutters" are those people who rely on other methods besides cable to get their entertainment fix.

Cord cutting is most common among millennials. About one in four Canadians between the ages of 18 and 24 says they are a cord cutter. Meanwhile, about 15% of those over age 35 say they've cut the cord. Cord cutting has soared in recent years—2015 alone saw an 80% increase in cord cutting over 2014.[3] The cable companies have responded by introducing "skinny" plans and pick-and-pay, but so far it remains to be seen if it will stop the bleeding.

I considered cable a necessity until I lived on my own. My parents had always grumbled about the cable bill. This got me thinking, do I really need cable? I decided to go without cable when I moved into my house and see how long I could last. Four years later I'm still cable-free, with no regrets.

But if you go cable-free, the last thing you want to do is stare at a blank TV screen. Here are cable alternatives to still get your entertainment fix.

HD Antenna

When you think of TV antennas, you probably picture rabbit ears on your old black-and-white. Fortunately, TV antennas have come a long way since the old days. Over a million Canadians watch TV using an antenna instead of paying for cable.[4] With a decent HD (high definition) antenna, you may be able to get more than 20 channels over the air. They won't work for every home, though. Before investing in one, make sure you have a clear view. Visit TVFool.com for a list of channels you're likely to receive.

Installing a HD antenna is the perfect DIY project—if you have a ladder and you're comfortable going up onto the roof, it should be no sweat. And $100 for a decent HD antenna and $75 for supplies pretty much pays for itself after a couple of months of living cable-free. If you don't feel comfortable being up on the roof, hire a company to install it—the installation cost is usually between $300 and $700 for parts and labour. Be sure to get two to three quotes for the work.

Streaming: Netflix and Apple TV

If you have high-speed Internet, take advantage of it. You'll find lots of videos on the Internet, and some TV networks let you stream shows online for free. And for about $10 a month, Netflix is a no-brainer—watch your favourite shows commercial-free.

I know what you're thinking—*I don't want to sit in front of my laptop for hours on end!* You don't have to. There are simple and inexpensive ways to stream content to your TV. You can plug your laptop into your TV with an HDMI cable, or go wireless. Smart TVs, Blu-ray players and gaming consoles also offer access to streaming services like Netflix- and CraveTV. Other streaming options are Apple TV, Chromecast and Roku, to name a few.

Save on Your Phone

We love our smartphones. Two-thirds (67%) of Canadians owned a smartphone in 2015.[5] We also pay some of the highest rates in the industrialized world. Canadians spend on average of $56 per month or almost $700 per year on their smartphones.[6]

If you're fed up with high cell-phone bills, you're not alone. Here are simple ways to save on your cell phone.

- **See what else is out there.** If you're always keeping under your available minutes, see if there's a cheaper plan with your current provider. If your contract is nearing the end of its term, shop around. Consider other providers besides the "big three"—Bell, Rogers and Telus. With some discount providers, you'll get more for less (read customer reviews before signing up, as the reception may not be the greatest).

- **Switch to a prepaid plan.** If you rarely make voice calls, mostly texting instead, consider switching to a prepaid plan. I did and saved big time. Now I pay only $100 for an entire year of unlimited texting and 100 minutes. Switching to prepaid doesn't make sense for everyone. If you use a lot of data on your favourite apps, you may be better off with a monthly plan.

- **Bundle and save.** See if you can bundle your cell-phone plan with your cable and Internet. Many service providers offer a bundling discount when you sign a two- or three-year contact. Bundling is a good way to save as long as you don't break your contract, as the termination fee can be hefty.

- **Share your plan.** Many carriers let you share a plan. Typically, you pay a flat monthly rate for voice and data that's shared among your family. Depending on your family's usage, the savings can be substantial. Before making the switch, look at each person's usage and see if sharing a plan makes sense for you. Also make sure to sign up for a plan with sufficient voice and data to avoid paying overage charges.

- **Watch your data usage.** Cell-phone data overage charges can be costly. Try to avoid data-heavy apps like Netflix and YouTube, which will blow through your phone's data in a New York minute. Turn off the data on all your apps when you're not using them. Save your data by using free Wi-Fi when possible at coffee shops, restaurants and airports.

- **Ask for a better deal.** Tired of paying sky-high cell-phone bills? Call your carrier and see what it can do for you. You may be offered a one-time promo or be able to switch to a less costly plan. If you're not getting anywhere with the customer service rep, ask to speak to the retention department. Mention you're unhappy with your plan and thinking of switching.

magicJack GO

If you're looking to save on cell-phone minutes and long-distance charges, consider using magicJack GO. I use magicJack GO as my home phone. For about $35 a year (less than most people pay per *month* for their cell phone), I get a local phone number and unlimited long-distance calling within Canada and the U.S. To use magicJack GO, all you need is a computer with high-speed Internet. To take your number with you, download magicApp, to make and receive calls over Wi-Fi on your cell phone.

Free Cell-Phone Service

Why pay for cell-phone service when you don't have to? Join the growing number of Canadians no longer paying for a monthly plan. Mobile apps like Fongo and TextNow let you make calls across Canada for free using Wi-Fi access or data connection. Enjoy features likes voicemail and call display at no extra charge. Once you sign up, you get a new phone number for free, or you can transfer your existing phone number for a small one-time fee. If you talk frequently on the phone, you may not want to cancel your plan, but you can at least use the apps as a backup to save on your minutes.

• • • • •

5 Key Mortgage-Burning Takeaways

➤ **Save on groceries.** Food is the second-highest monthly expense after mortgage or rent for most families. Shaving a few dollars off your grocery bill every week can really add up.

➤ **Be a smart shopper.** Consider shopping at discount supermarkets, buy in bulk and price match to save money.

➤ **Avoid impulse buys.** Make a shopping list, and avoid shopping on an empty stomach. Don't browse the entire store; just visit the aisles you need to.

➤ **Cut the cord.** Ditch cable TV and save a bundle. Use TV alternatives like a Netflix and a HD antenna.

➤ **Save on your cell phone.** Don't be afraid to ask your provider for a better deal. Shop around for a plan that better suits your needs. To save on minutes, use magicJack GO and a free cell-phone service.

The best car safety device is a rear-view
mirror with a cop in it.
DUDLEY MOORE, actor

6

Getting from Point A to Point B for Less
Trimming Transportation Costs

ACHIEVING FINANCIAL FREEDOM is all about trade-offs. In cities with sky-high real estate prices, it can be tough to afford a home, let alone a car, and have any money left over to enjoy yourself. If you can get by without owning a car, it can really help your pocketbook (I know you love your car, but hear me out). You can save thousands of dollars a year by not owning a car—money to put toward your mortgage.

Going carless makes sense for some people, but it's not practical for everyone. If you have kids, taking them to daycare, picking them up from soccer practice and running daily errands is a lot easier with a car. Likewise, if your total daily commute is more than two hours, driving probably makes sense. So you might not be able to go carless, but if you have two cars, could you get away with having only one? You *don't* need to sweat the small stuff like the odd Starbucks coffees, but you *do* need to be smart on big purchases like a car.

In this chapter we'll look at the costs associated with owning a car, along with practical ways to save. I'll also offer tips on how to buy a car for less. If you live in an urban centre and use a car only occasionally, maybe it's time to investigate car-sharing services. Or have you considered cycling? You'll read more about commuting on two wheels below.

The True Price of Owning a Car (It's More Than You May Think)

Homeownership rates are high in Canada, but they're nothing compared with car ownership rates. According to Statistics Canada, about 69% of Canadians own a home.[1] Meanwhile, 83% of Canadians own a vehicle.[2]

Cars don't come cheap. Canadians spend an average of $26,044 when buying a new vehicle. Operating a vehicle isn't cheap either—Canadians spend an average of $5,250 a year on vehicle-related expenses, including payments, insurance, fuel and maintenance. Let's take a closer look at the expenses, along with ways to save.

Auto Insurance

The cost of home insurance is a drop in the bucket compared with how much you'll shell out to protect your car. This makes sense, since you're probably more likely to make a claim on your auto insurance than on your home insurance. Your auto insurance premium depends on several factors, including the car's make and model, your driving record, and your deductible and type of coverage.

Registration and Licence

Before you can drive your brand-new, shiny car off the lot, you'll need vehicle registration (usually the dealer helps you with this). If you're buying a used car, you may have a few days in which to obtain the registration. In some provinces, emissions tests are mandatory for older cars, adding to your costs. Save time by renewing your driver's licence online, and pay with your credit card to earn cash back or reward points.

Fuel

Your car won't drive itself. You'll need fuel to power the engine (unless you have an electric car). Although you can choose to drive your car less often, if you live in the suburbs, you may have a lengthy commute to work, and you'll be at the mercy of the price at the pumps. By taking your car in for regular tune-ups and driving at a steady speed, you can make your tank of fuel go further. For more ways to save, read *75 Ways to Save Gas* by Jim Davidson.

Electric Cars

Looking to save on fuel and help the environment? Electric cars are worth considering. Tesla Motors has taken the car industry by storm with its electric models. Electric cars typically come at a higher price tag than conventional fuel-powered cars, so to help reduce greenhouse emissions and encourage the shift to low- and zero-emission cars, some provinces—B.C., Ontario and Quebec—are offering financial incentives. You may be eligible for rebates when buying or leasing an electric car or installing a home charging system.

Electric cars probably aren't practical if you live in a small town (this should be less of a problem if electric cars really catch on), but if you live in a large city with plenty of charging stations, consider making the switch.

Five Easy Ways to Save on Auto Insurance

1 Buy a vehicle with insurance costs in mind. Find out about premiums before you buy. Look for a make and model that will translate into a lower insurance premium.
2 Bundle your home and auto insurance. Many insurance providers offer a sizable discount when you have both policies with them.
3 Shop around. When your policy comes up for renewal, take the time to shop the market. A lower rate could mean saving thousands over the life of your vehicle. Websites like Kanetix.ca make it easier than ever to compare rates.
4 Pay yearly. Auto insurance companies often offer a discount for paying your premium once a year on renewal instead of through monthly payments. Coming up with the full premium at once can be tough. To make budgeting easier, set up a dedicated savings account and save up ahead of time.
5 Raise your deductible. Consider upping your deductible. The savings on your premium can add up over time. Put extra emergency savings aside to protect yourself in the event of an accident.

Maintenance and Repairs

Your car needs regular maintenance and repairs to keep it in tip-top shape. Not only can skipping regular tune-ups and maintenance on your car cost you more in the long term, it can put everyone on the road in danger.

Be sure to have money set aside in your emergency fund for unexpected car repairs. You never know when your car's going to break down on the road. If you drive frequently, CAA (Canadian Automobile Association) memberships can come in handy, especially for towing and battery boosts.

Free Roadside Assistance
Before you sign up for a CAA membership, check to see if you already have free roadside assistance through your credit card. There's no point in paying for coverage twice.

Parking

If your home doesn't have a driveway or garage, you may need to shell out money for a street parking permit. Ditto for parking lot and meter fees when you're out and about. Use parking apps like BestParking to find free and inexpensive parking spots.

Depreciation

You've probably heard that a car loses much of its value the moment it's driven off the lot—that's depreciation, folks. Unlike the family home, which typically goes up in value, a vehicle is a depreciating asset. As your car gets older, it loses its value—often at an alarming rate. Unless it's a vintage car, you probably won't get anywhere near the sticker price when you resell it. To save on depreciation, consider buying used (see How to Buy a Car for Less, below).

Financing

Since a car is a depreciating asset, try to save up ahead of time for it—see Good Debt vs. Not-So-Good (Bad) Debt, below. Set up a dedicated car savings account and put some money, say, $300, in it from every paycheque.

If you don't have the extra cash sitting around and you need a car now, you'll need to borrow the money. Carefully weigh the pros and cons of a car loan versus leasing to see what makes the most sense.

Good Debt vs. Not-So-Good (Bad) Debt

Similar to cholesterol, debt has two types: good and bad. Good debt is any money you borrow for something likely to increase your net worth—borrowing for a home or postsecondary education and investing, for instance. Bad debt is any money borrowed for something that's goes down in value (a car or clothes) or is used up immediately (a vacation). A car by definition is bad debt, though there are ways to lessen its impact on your family's finances, such as saving on the auto insurance premium.

The distinction between good debt and bad debt isn't always black and white. Just like the animals in the reality TV show *When Good Pets Go Bad*, good debt sometimes goes bad (unfortunately, I have yet to see bad debt go good). Buying a home you can't afford, getting a university degree but having few job prospects and buying a risky investment that tanks are all examples of bad debt. Try to avoid them at all costs.

How to Buy a Car for Less

Just because you've decided to buy a car doesn't mean you have to spend a small fortune. In the book *The Millionaire Next Door*, authors Thomas Stanley and William Danko reveal that most millionaires don't drive top-of-the-line cars—they drive economical cars. Most millionaires also own their cars, rather than leasing them. Also, a third of millionaires buy used cars instead of new.[3] The brand of choice? Not a flashy BMW—a reliable and affordable Toyota.

Four Ways to Save Money on a Car

1 **Set a budget.** Create a budget and stick to it. Choose a make and model you can afford. Don't forget about the costs beyond the sticker price, such as auto insurance, maintenance and fuel.

2 **Sell your old car on your own.** Car dealerships make it convenient to trade in your old vehicle, but by doing that you're liking leaving money on the table. If you have the time and your old car is in decent shape, consider selling it on a website like autoTRADER.

3 **Buy used.** To avoid taking the hit of depreciation, buy a used car. Look for a two- to three-year-old used car with low mileage. Consider buying from a registered new-car dealer; this is typically a lot safer than private sales, which may be an attempt to offload a stolen vehicle.

4 **Do your homework.** If you're buying a used vehicle, request the vehicle's ownership history. Get a car inspection done. Make sure it hasn't been involved in any major accidents and doesn't have any liens against it.

The Car-Sharing Economy

If you only need a car occasionally, you may be best off using a car-sharing service. It offers the perfect middle ground between owning a vehicle and not owning a vehicle. You're no longer paying for a car to sit in your driveway, and you save on the ongoing expenses of owning a car.

The big car-sharing services in Canada are Zipcar, Enterprise Car-Share and car2go. Each offers a different plan; see which one suits your needs. Zipcar and Enterprise are similar: an annual membership fee, plus an hourly rate, and you may book vehicles in advance. With car2go, you can't book vehicles ahead of time, but you can drop them off at any designated parking lot, making them ideal for one-way trips (maybe grab an Uber ride home).

Cycle and Save a Bundle

If you're looking to dramatically reduce your transportation costs, look no further than the bicycle. I've managed to get by quite nicely without ever owning a car. I ride my bike nine months out of the year—between April and December. During winter, I take public transit. I estimate I save almost $5,000 a year by cycling instead of driving. With this extra money, I was able to save toward my down payment and pay off my mortgage faster.

Cycling has many benefits. If you live in a big city and close to your work, cycling can be a great way to quickly get around (it sure beats the heck out of being packed like sardines on the bus or being stuck in a traffic jam during rush hour). Not only can cycling help you be more productive at work (you'll feel energized from the work-out), it's a good way to stay in shape. But cycling doesn't make sense for everyone. As I mentioned, if you live in the suburbs, you may be better off with a car (but there's nothing stopping you from running errands on your bike).

Interested in trading in your four wheels for two? Here's what you need to know about cycling.

Bicycle and Gear

The start-up costs of biking to work are relatively low compared with those of a car. I suggest spending $500 on a decent bicycle for commuting. You don't want a flashy bike that's a target for thieves, but you also don't want one that's so cheap it continually breaks down. A good bike lock is a must. Fenders are helpful so you don't end up covered in mud on rainy days, as are a rear rack and bike bags to carry your belongings.

Save Money by Bike Sharing

Consider signing up for bike-sharing programs in big cities like Toronto and Vancouver. They're a great way to save on maintenance and repairs. In Toronto, the annual fee is under $100 (less than the cost of a monthly transit pass) for unlimited 30-minute trips.

You don't need to dress from head to toe in spandex to cycle, but there is some basic gear. Cycling gloves reduce blisters, keep your hands warm and prevent them from going numb on long rides. Cuff clips keep your pants from being caught in the bike chain. Cycling gear at local bike shops can be expensive; outdoor recreation stores often have a good selection at reasonable prices.

If you'll be riding in the rain, be sure to pick up a waterproof coat and pants, and shoe covers to keep your feet dry. Look for high-quality material like Gore-Tex. If you'll be riding during winter, pick up a bike just for that (it's not worth ruining your $500 bike just to save $300 on transit). You can often find inexpensive bikes at the local bike shop, or look on Kijiji or Craigslist. Other essential bike gear includes a helmet, front and rear lights for night riding, a tool kit and a bike pump.

Maintenance and Repairs

As with a car, it's important to take good care of a bike. Sign up for a maintenance workshop (many neighbourhood bike shops and universities offer them) so you know at least the basics.

A $60 tune-up in the spring is money well spent (or do it yourself, if you've taken a bike maintenance course). You can also expect to spend about $60 a year on flat-tire repair (three flats) and $50 to replace worn parts. That's a grand total of only $170 per year. That sure beats the annual price tag of over $5,000 for owning a car.

● ● ● ● ●

5 Key Mortgage-Burning Takeaways

➤ **Consider going carless.** On average, Canadians spend over $5,000 each year on their car. If it's practical, lose the car, and bike, walk or take transit instead.

➤ **Save on auto insurance.** Combine your home and auto insurance, raise your deductible and shop around on renewal to lower your premiums.

➤ **Distinguish between good and bad debt.** Good debt is for anything likely to go up in value, like a home. Bad debt is anything that goes down in value, like a car.

➤ **Buy a used car or car share.** Let someone else drive the brand-new car off the lot and lose half its value. Buy a two- to three-year-old used car from a reputable dealer. If you need a vehicle only occasionally, use a car-sharing service.

➤ **Invest in a decent bike.** Buy a decent bike for commuting. If you'll be riding in winter weather, buy a less expensive bike just for those months.

The art is not in making money, but in keeping it.
PROVERB

7

Coming Up with Your Down Payment
How to Become a Super Saver

THE EASIEST WAY to avoid a massive mortgage is to make a hefty down payment, yet with home prices heading into the stratosphere, saving for a down payment in many cities can seem daunting. I feel your pain. I bought a home in Toronto, Canada's second most expensive housing market, where the average price of a detached house is over $1 million.

If you've already saved up your down payment, bravo! You're that much closer to being a homeowner. If you're already a homeowner, even bigger kudos. For everyone else, you'll need to save up enough for a down payment. But don't worry, I'll show you how to become a super saver, to get there sooner.

Before saving for a down payment, try to clear up your consumer debt. It hardly makes sense to save for a down payment when you're paying 18% interest on your credit card. Ideally, you're debt-free when you start saving toward a down payment, but that just isn't realistic these days. Many people have student debt and car loans to deal with.

If you have student debt or a car loan on its last legs, focus on paying that off first. Once your debt is paid off, take the money you were putting toward debt repayment and pay yourself first (more on this concept below). But if you have low-interest debt you're years away from paying off, it makes sense to keep paying down your debt while starting to save toward a home. The last thing you want is to find yourself priced out of the market.

Should You Buy Now or Later? Getting Priced Out of the Market

You've probably heard the term "priced out of the market" tossed about like a salad, but do you really know what it means? It means no longer being able to afford a home in your desired location because real estate prices have gone up faster than you can save. Potential homebuyers in seller's markets know the feeling all too well—here, you can lose out on your dream home simply by sitting on the sidelines.

The shortage of listings is leading to buyer gridlock. Entry-level homeowners are choosing to stay put and renovate their homes instead of upsizing to a bigger home. And starter homes are in short supply, pushing prices even higher.

Let's say you wanted to buy a home for $500,000 (a nice round number). If home prices go up 10% in the next year (which is quite possible in big cities like Toronto),

Buy a Home When You're Financially Ready

Some homebuyers have sat on the sidelines for years, hoping home prices will come crashing down. Instead, they've watched home prices go even higher. Real estate is a long-term investment. Everyone needs a place to live. When you're financially ready to buy, start housing hunting.

the home that once cost $500,000 now costs $550,000. That's a $50,000 price increase in a year—yikes! If you weren't able to save at least $50,000, your home-buying power would fall. In a couple of years, instead of being able to afford a spacious three-bedroom house, you might only be able to afford a cramped two-bedroom house. If prices keep going up at this pace, you might only be able to afford a one-bedroom condo. This isn't a fun situation to be in.

The Impact of Foreign Buyers

The Canadian real estate market is a popular place for foreign buyers to invest. It's not hard to see why—our real estate market is seen as a safe place for foreign investors. The Vancouver real estate market especially has seen an influx of buyers from overseas with deep pockets. But their impact is also being felt in Toronto's downtown condo market. It's estimated that 10% of new condos being built in central Toronto are being bought by foreign buyers.[1]

Although foreign buyers help prop up the economy, many locals are finding themselves being priced out of the market. It's probably wise, if you're in the financial position to do so, to buy now while you can still afford to.

Turning to the Bank of Mom and Dad

If you're buying in a high-priced market like Toronto and Vancouver, I feel your pain. Buying a condo, let alone a house, in these cities is tough. That's why many first-time homebuyers are turning to the Bank of Mom and Dad. Forty-two percent of first-timer homebuyers get help with their down payment from family.[2] Many parents are willing to help out if it means their adult kids will be able to buy in a decent neighbourhood close by. Where are parents getting the money from? Many are tapping into the equity they've built up in their homes with a home equity line of credit (HELOC).

Mom and Dad as Co-applicants
If you're having trouble qualifying for a mortgage (maybe you're self-employed or lack a credit history), your parents can help, as a co-applicant. Under this arrangement, your parents essentially buy the home with you. They're on the title and mortgage for income or credit help.

While there's no shame in asking for help, to better your chances of making a successful withdrawal from the Bank of Mom and Dad, go prepared. Save as much toward your down payment on your own as you can. If you've made the effort, your parents may be more willing to top up your down payment to avoid your having to pay a mortgage insurance premium (more on this below).

Your parents can help you with your down payment in several ways. They can gift you the money outright, with no strings attached. Or they can arrange a living inheritance, whereby they gift you your inheritance now, while they're still alive. This is an emerging trend in Canada—61% of baby boomers plan to pass on money to their children during their lifetime.[3]

Buying with Family and Friends

An emerging trend among young buyers is purchasing real estate with family and friends: one in four millennials would consider buying a home with a friend, and 24% would consider buying with a family member.[4] This is most common in high-priced markets, where it might take years to save up a down payment.

Buying with family and friends can be a great way to build equity and get your foot in the door. You don't even have to live together— some people do it purely as an investment.

When buying a property with someone, treat it like a business. Work with a lawyer to draft a plan in the event that one person wants to sell. Also consider the pain and strain owning such a large asset can put on your relationship. If your co-buyer loses their job and can't pay the mortgage, this may end up hurting *your* credit score.

Saving for a Down Payment

The down payment is what stops many people from making the jump from renter to homeowner. In Canada, the minimum down payment on a home can be as little as 5%. That may not sound like much, but with the average price of a detached home over $1 million in Toronto and Vancouver, it can actually be a lot. For example, on a $500,000 home, the minimum down payment is $25,000.

I started saving toward my down payment even before I graduated from college. By working three part-time jobs and full time in the summer, I graduated debt-free with a net worth of $70,000. After graduating, I lived in my mother's basement (and again, no, it wasn't rent-free—I paid my mother $600 a month). I was a super saver—I saved over 70% of my income. I was disciplined—any "found" money, like bonuses, cash gifts, pay raises and tax refunds, instead of spending, I saved. In my spare time, I worked as a personal finance journalist.

When I bought my home three years later, I made a sizable down payment of $170,000 (and no, my parents didn't help me with my down payment). I know $100,000 is a lot to save in three years, but I was focused and made decent money from side hustle (see the appendix). I was able to save this much because I buckled down and did what it took to save.

So how much should you save for your down payment? Should you save the minimum down payment (5% for a purchase price under $500,000; when the purchase price is between $500,000 and $1 million, 5% on the first $500,000 and 10% for the portion above), or should you save 20%? If you're in a small or midsize city like Regina or Winnipeg, where real estate is still affordable, aim for a 20% down payment. But if you're in a major city where home prices keep rising, you're generally better off buying when you've saved the minimum down payment (aim for a 10% down payment instead of 5%, to save on mortgage insurance). If you're on the cusp of saving 20%, it's probably worth waiting until you can save at least 20% to avoid costly mortgage insurance. Just make sure you aren't priced out of the market while you're saving.

Hard Work Pays Off

I met a woman named Jennifer who had bought a preconstruction condo four years earlier, when she was 20 years old. Jennifer had always wanted to own her own home. On top of working full time as a legal assistant, she serves part time at a restaurant and goes to school two nights a week, studying to get a law clerk certificate. She usually works 65 hours a week. This has given her a great appreciation for both time and money. Hard work pays off—after saving enough for a down payment, Jennifer recently moved into her condo and is starting her journey toward mortgage freedom.

Pay Yourself First

Unless you're a super saver at heart like me, you might find it challenging to save up enough for a down payment. Don't give up—there's hope! There's a trick to make saving that much easier called "pay yourself first." So how much do you save? From the goal-setting exercise in chapter 1, you will already have an idea about how much money you'll need to save each month for your dream home. Let's say you want to save $30,000 in three years—that's a lot of dough! But when you break it down, it doesn't seem so bad. That's $10,000 per year, or only $417 twice a month. If you're living rent-free at home, you should have no problem saving this. For those not living at home, try to save as much as you can afford. Take a close look at your budget and look for ways to cut back without crimping your lifestyle (see chapter 2 for ideas).

There are two ways to pay yourself first. The easiest is through direct deposit. Many employers let you set things up so your paycheque is automatically deposited into your bank account—it doesn't get any easier than that!

If your employer doesn't offer that, or you're self-employed, set up preauthorized transfers from your primary bank account to a dedicated high-interest savings account. Have the money transferred the day after you're paid or on some other regular basis, so you're not tempted to spend it. Once you get into the good habit of paying yourself first, you'll be well on your way to buying your dream home.

Mortgage Insurance: Avoid It If You Can

If your down payment is less than 20%, you're required by Canadian mortgage rules to purchase high-ratio mortgage insurance (not to be confused with mortgage life insurance). Unlike home insurance, high-ratio mortgage insurance doesn't protect your *home*, it protects your *lender* should you fail to pay (i.e., default on) your mortgage. Your mortgage insurance premium will depend on how hefty your down payment is (the closer it is to 20%, the lower the premium percentage). The premium may be paid as a lump sum, though most homeowners choose to add it to their mortgage (if you were flush with cash, you'd probably make a larger down payment).

Here's a table of mortgage insurance premiums.*

Down payment tiers (%)	Mortgage insurance premium (%)
Tier 1: 5 to 9.99	3.60
Tier 2: 10 to 14.99	2.40
Tier 3: 15 to 19.99	1.80
Tier 4: 20 or higher	0.00

* Premiums current as of June 1, 2015, and are subject to change (the government likes to tweak the rules from time to time). Before you buy, check the CHMC (Canada Mortgage and Housing Corporation) website for up-to-date premiums.

EXAMPLE THE POWER OF SAVING

Mortgage insurance can help you buy a home sooner, but it can end up costing you dearly. Homeowners often don't realize how costly mortgage insurance can be. It's helpful to think of your down payment in tiers, as outlined above. The table below shows the difference in mortgage insurance premiums between 9% down and 10% down on a $375,000 condo.

	Tier 1 ($): 9% down (3.6% premium)	Tier 2 ($): 10% down (2.4% premium)
Purchase price	375,000	375,000
Down payment	33,750	37,500
Mortgage (before mortgage insurance)	341,250	337,500
Mortgage insurance	12,285	8,100
Mortgage insurance saved	0	4,185

By scraping together a slightly higher down payment (tier 2; $3,750 more), you'll save $4,185 on your mortgage insurance premium. Try finding a better return on investment anywhere else! If you're on the cusp of reaching the next down payment tier, buckle down and do what it takes to reach it (or if you can't save up enough, consider buying a slightly less expensive home). Try to avoid the first tier (5% to 9.99%) at all cost, as the premium is costly.

We haven't even factored in the amount of interest you'll save over the life of your mortgage. In tier 1, a *smaller* down payment and *higher* mortgage insurance premium, you'll have a mortgage of $353,535

($341,250 + $12,285), but in tier 2, a slightly *higher* down payment and *lower* mortgage insurance premium, you'll have a mortgage of only $345,600 ($337,500 + $8,100), $7,935 lower. Assuming a 2.99% fixed-rate mortgage paid monthly over 25 years, you'll save $8,547 in interest and pay off your mortgage nine months earlier with a slightly higher down payment.

Three Ways to Supercharge Your Down Payment

Buying in a pricey real estate market? Here are three ways to save a down payment sooner:

1 Move in with the 'rents. It's tough to save a down payment when you're paying big-city rent. By living at home rent-free or with below-market rent, you can maximize your savings. Your parents may not be too keen on this, so remind them it's only temporary. In lieu of paying rent, offer to help out around the house.

2 Downsize to a bachelor pad. If you have a one- or two-bedroom apartment, downsize to a bachelor apartment. You might also consider renting in a less pricey part of town.

3 Split the rent with a roommate. Roommates aren't just for students. If you aren't ready to forgo your upscale downtown condo, share the rent with a roommate. To save even more, consider renting a one-bedroom condo with a den that can be used as a bedroom.

Where to Park Your Money So It Grows Faster, Safely

Saving your money is only half the battle. You also want that money to grow. The sooner you save enough money, the sooner you'll be living in your dream home. If you're planning to buy a home in the next five years, stay clear of riskier investments like mutual funds and exchange-traded funds (ETFs). Sure you can earn a higher return, but you can also lose a bundle. The last thing you want is to lose half your down payment when the market decides to take a nose dive just days before your closing date. Here are safe places to park your money yet also help it grow.

High-Interest Savings Accounts

Savings accounts offer the most flexible and easiest way to save toward your down payment. If you want to save $800 per month, you can have the money transferred automatically from your chequing or other account to your dedicated savings account lickety-split—before you're tempted to spend it (see Pay Yourself First, above).

GICs

If you're looking for a safe investment, look no further than GICs (guaranteed investment certificates). Unlike with stocks and mutual funds, the money you invest in GICs is guaranteed. You can expect to get back your original investment, plus interest. Your money is locked up for a set period (anywhere from 90 days to 10 years). Usually, the longer your money is locked up, the higher the interest rate you'll get.

Spread your investment risk and boost your investment return with a GIC ladder. If you have $9,000 to invest, for example, instead of buying a $9,000 three-year GIC at 1.7%, buy a $3,000 one-year GIC at 1.4%, a $3,000 two-year GIC at 1.6% and a $3,000 three-year GIC at 1.7%. Each year that your GICs mature, buy a longer-term GIC (hopefully) at a higher rate.

RRSP Home Buyers' Plan (HBP)

There's no simpler, more powerful way to boost your down payment than with the Home Buyers' Plan, or HBP. Under the HBP, first-time homebuyers can borrow up to $25,000 tax-free from their Registered Retirement Savings Plan (RRSP) for a down payment. (If you're buying with another first-time homebuyer, that's a total of $50,000 you can borrow together.)

Don't confuse the RRSP with investment vehicles like stocks and bonds. The RRSP is a tax-sheltered account that can hold a variety of investments, including savings accounts and GICs. You may contribute the lesser of 18% of your earned income from the previous year or the RRSP limit for the current tax year.

What makes the RRSP so powerful is that you'll get a tax refund for your contributions. For example, if your tax rate is 30%, by contributing $10,000 to your RRSP, you'll get a 30% tax refund (effectively

$3,000)—that's a 30% return on your money! (The size of your refund depends on your tax situation. You may get more or less back depending on your personal tax rate.)

If you decide to use the HBP, follow the rules to the letter. Money borrowed under the HBP must be fully repaid within 15 years, with payments starting in the second year. If you fail to repay any amount, not only is it added back to your income as taxable (ouch!), but you lose the RRSP contribution room forever (double ouch!).

Some financial experts say that using the HBP isn't a good idea because you're borrowing money from your future self, and you'll never get back the lost compound interest. That may be true, but in this crazy real estate market where home prices are rising a lot faster than wages, it's hard to turn down a 30% risk-free return. The HBP makes sense for a couple of more reasons: (1) most Canadians have more RRSP contribution room than they know what to do with, and (2) you'll save a boatload on your mortgage insurance premium if your mortgage is high ratio by making a larger down payment.

Tax-Free Savings Account (TFSA)

If you're not a first-time homebuyer, the tax-free savings account (TFSA) is your best bet. Similar to the RRSP, the TFSA is a tax-sheltered account that can hold investments like GICs and saving accounts, making it perfect for long-term savings goals such as homeownership. Anyone who's 18 or older can open and contribute to a TFSA.

Unlike the RRSP, you don't get a tax refund from TFSA contributions, but similar to the RRSP, your money grows tax-free inside it. Where the TFSA has a leg up on the RRSP is that you don't have to pay income tax when you withdraw your money. The TFSA was introduced way back in 2009, so you should have plenty of contribution room for saving toward your dream home.

EXAMPLE BATTLE OF THE TAX-SHELTERED ACCOUNTS: RRSP VS. TFSA
Using the earlier example of a tax rate of 30% and a $10,000 RRSP contribution, you're $3,000 ahead by contributing to your RRSP instead of to a TFSA. Since you'd like to buy a home in three years, if you're a first-time homebuyer, you're better off contributing to your RRSP.

	TFSA ($)	RRSP ($)
Contribution	10,000	10,000
Tax refund (30% tax rate)	0	3,000
Total	**10,000**	**13,000**

• • • • •

5 Key Mortgage-Burning Takeaways

➤ **Don't get priced out of the market.** In some cities, home prices go up faster than you can save. After a year or two, you may no longer be able to afford your dream home. Purchase a home as soon as you're financially ready.

➤ **Visit the Bank of Mom and Dad.** There's no shame in asking your parents for help, especially in pricey real estate markets. Common ways for parents to help out include gifting a portion of your down payment and being a co-applicant on your mortgage.

➤ **Save on mortgage insurance.** Mortgage insurance is costly. It can add thousands of dollars in interest over the life of your mortgage. Try to save at least a 20% down payment to avoid paying it altogether.

➤ **Pay yourself first.** Avoid the temptation to spend. Make saving automatic via direct deposit or preauthorized transfers to your dedicated savings account.

➤ **Grow your down payment faster.** If you're a first-time homebuyer, take advantage of the RRSP Home Buyers' Plan. For everyone else, the TFSA is the best place to save.

Part 2

The Buy

To build true long-term wealth, you must
buy and hold real estate.
WARREN BUFFETT, business magnate

8

Home-Buying Basics
Surviving and Thriving
in Today's Real Estate Jungle

PICTURE IT NOW, your dream home. Mine is a mansion in Beverly Hills, with the whole nine yards. We're talking tennis court, circular drive and helicopter landing pad. (In case you're wondering, a bungalow in Toronto was my close second choice.) Whatever your dream home looks like, it's time to see if you have the money to make your dreams a reality.

Buying a home is a good long-term investment—most of the time. But it doesn't always make good sense. (With a book title like *Burn Your Mortgage*, I bet you weren't expecting me to say that.) In fact, you may jeopardize your financial freedom if you buy a home before you're ready to and end up selling it within a year, say. This chapter starts by looking at whether you're ready to buy a home.

Once you have decided homeownership *is* right for you, it's time to go house hunting. It's often said that the three most important things in real estate are location, location, location. That may be true, but there are other things to consider too. Homebuyers today are faced with more choices than a menu at McDonald's—house or condo, urban or suburban, eat in or take out (well, maybe just the first two). This can seem intimating, but it doesn't have to be. I break down the home-buying process step by step, to make it simpler and stress-free. Before you know it, you'll be able to proudly call yourself a homeowner.

Are You Ready to Buy a Home?

Homeownership is a great long-term investment for many people. But sometimes it makes more sense to rent until you're financially ready to buy a home.

If you're buying on a shoestring budget with 5% down at the maximum purchase price approved by your lender, you're probably better off renting a while longer. This will let you save up a larger down payment and an emergency fund, so you're not strapped for cash and within a mortgage payment of losing the home you've worked so hard to buy.

Are you still on the fence about buying? Here are important things to consider when deciding whether you're ready to buy.

Buying

Pros

- **Forced savings:** Most people put their mortgage ahead of all other debts, and for good reason—if you stop paying your mortgage, you'll no longer have a roof over your head.

- **Good debt (most of the time):** When you buy a home, you're investing in something that is likely to go up in value (in the world of finance, it's known as an *appreciating asset*). One day you'll (hopefully) be mortgage-free.

- **Income:** A home isn't just a place to live. If your home has a basement suite or is a duplex, rent out the unit and pay down your mortgage even faster (more on this in chapter 14).

- **Leveraging:** Leveraging means you're borrowing someone else's money (the bank's) to buy an asset (a home). If all goes according to plan, you'll pay off your mortgage, and with the likely rise in real estate prices, your home will be worth a lot more.

- **Freedom and privacy:** You don't have to ask the landlord for permission to paint or landscape (you own the place).

- **Tax credits:** If you're a first-time homebuyer, you can claim the home buyers' tax credit (HBTC). This non-refundable tax credit is based on an amount of $5,000 multiplied by the lowest personal income tax rate (15% in 2016). In 2016, you'd pocket about $750 by claiming this credit. If you're buying a new home for less than $450,000 and it's your principal residence, you may qualify for the GST/HST new housing rebate, as well.

- **Tax shelter:** In most cases when you sell your principal residence, you won't have to pay a dime in taxes on the gain in value of the home (although if you rent out part of your home or have a home-based business and claim capital cost allowances, you may have to pay capital gains tax).

- **Home equity:** Once you've built up some equity by paying down your mortgage, you can tap into your home's value and borrow at a super-cheap rate with a HELOC.

Cons
- **Closing costs:** Unless you're planning to stay put for five years or longer, you're generally better off renting. Closing costs from buying and selling your home can easily wipe out any gains you made from buying.

- **Carrying costs:** On top of your mortgage payments, you'll have to fork over money for utilities, property tax and home insurance. These carrying costs have a habit of rising a lot faster than your paycheque.

- **Maintenance and repairs:** Over the years, you'll have to spend mega bucks on a new roof, furnace, windows . . . the list goes on. Budget from 3% to 5% of your home's value for these costs. For a $500,000 home, that's up to $25,000 each year.

Take time to weigh these pros and cons. Buying or renting isn't just a financial decision, it's an emotional one. Consider all the factors and decide what's best for you.

Four Things to Consider Before Buying

1 How long do you plan to live there? If you don't plan to stay put for at least five years, you're likely better off renting.
2 What are your long-term plans? Are you planning to start a family? Would you mind relocating for a job promotion?
3 Can you afford a home? Before you start house hunting, get pre-approved for a mortgage to see how much home you can afford.
4 How will a home affect your monthly budget? Do up a budget as if you already owned the home and see how it would affect your lifestyle.

House, Townhouse or Condo?

Would you rather own a house, townhouse or condo? In pricey real estate markets like Toronto and Vancouver, you might not have a choice: all you may be able to afford is a condo. But for those buying in more affordable markets like Edmonton and Saskatoon, with a decent down payment, you'll have more choices.

For me, a house was the right choice. Although my lifestyle is better suited for a condo, I chose a house because I believe it's a better long-term investment than the other options. Here are factors to consider when choosing.

Moving to a New City? Consider Renting First

When moving to a new city, consider renting for the first few months. If you like it there, then buy. If you don't like it, you can always move somewhere else without the headache of selling a home.

House

A house offers a lot of freedom. Houses don't come with as many restrictions as do condos and townhouses—you're free to decorate the exterior, choose the window coverings and landscape pretty much as you see fit. A house frequently comes with a yard (perfect if you have children, or just to enjoy yourself). House prices tend to go up faster than condos and townhouses. And you can rent out part of your house, to help pay down the mortgage.

A house also comes with a lot more responsibilities. You'll have to mow the lawn (provided your lawn has grass) and shovel the snow (or pay someone to do it). Expect to spend more on home maintenance and repairs than if you owned a condo or townhouse (condo or association fees usually cover those). If you live a busy life or you're not particularly handy, you may be better off in a townhouse or condo.

Townhouse

A townhouse is a good compromise between a house and condo. The purchase price typically falls somewhere in between the two. Many townhouses are governed by a homeowners' association, which looks after maintenance and repairs, snow shovelling and yard work. Association fees may also cover amenities like a gym, swimming pool and tennis court. Security tends to be less of a concern than with a house, since your neighbours are close by.

Townhouses may not offer as much privacy as a house, since you're close to your neighbours. You also don't have as much freedom, as there are often restrictions on changes you can make to the interior and exterior. The yards of townhouses tend to be small—keep this in mind if you have a dog or like to entertain outdoors.

Condo

If a house is out of your price range, a condo may be the perfect fit. Condos are typically a lot more affordable than houses. You'll have a smaller mortgage and can pay it off sooner. With a condo, you won't have to worry about major repairs like a new roof or windows, since your condo fees cover those. Your condo fees also cover most utilities, and repairs and maintenance. This makes budgeting a lot easier. Other reasons to choose a condo include lifestyle preference, amenities and security.

When you own a condo and don't have a basement apartment, it's more difficult to "subsidize" your mortgage. You can get roommates, but you have to be comfortable sharing your personal space. Condos don't come with the same freedom as houses; there are often restrictions on everything from window coverings to pets. Your condo fees could skyrocket if the condo board is managing things poorly (not to mention that if you don't pay your condo fees, a lien can be put against your property). And if you receive special assessments—one-time fees for costly repairs not covered by the regular condo fees or contingency fund—you have no choice but to pay them.

If you don't mind living in cramped living quarters, a micro condo is an affordable option for single homebuyers in big cities. They're not for everyone—on average they're only 300 square feet (about the size of two parking spaces). They include space-saving features like a Murphy bed, movable wall panels and fold-out cabinetry. Think long and hard before buying a micro condo—you might have a tough time reselling it in a slower market. Some lenders are also hesitant to approve mortgages on them for this reason.

Location, Location, Location

We're often told that the most important thing when buying a home is location, location, location, but do you understand what that means exactly? It means homes can go up or down in value based on where they're located. (That's why some people buy fixer uppers in good neighbourhoods.)

Location, location, location is the number one rule in real estate, yet many buyers overlook it. You can improve your home in many ways. You can upgrade the flooring, renovate the kitchen and throw on a deck, but the one thing you can't change is the location. You could have the nicest house on the block, but if your neighbourhood is going downhill, you could have a tough time selling it.

Signs of a Good Location

- **Safe neighbourhood:** Before you buy, contact the local police department and ask about crime rates. You don't want to find out *after* moving in that your neighbour has already been burglarized twice this year.

- **Good schools:** This is especially important if you have children and for resale value. You'll want your kids to have a bright future.

- **Transportation:** Easy access to public transit and freeways is a bonus.

- **Amenities:** Look for a location close to desirable parks and amenities like restaurants and shopping.

- **View:** The view is especially important if you're buying a condo. It can be a key selling feature.

- **New developments:** Be on the lookout for new developments nearby, like condos. If neighbours are topping up their homes (adding a second-floor addition and redesigning the main floor), it's also a good sign.

Signs of a Poor Location

- **Undesirable factors:** Being too close to a fire station, a noisy schoolyard, railroad tracks or the freeway can hurt your home's resale value.

- **High crime rate:** Crime doesn't pay.

- **Lack of pride of ownership:** Are there lots of rental properties in the area? Are the homes and businesses run down?

Moving to the Suburbs? Factor in the Higher Transportation Costs
Although you might spend less on your home in the suburbs, you may have little choice but to buy a car. Make sure you consider the higher transportation cost.

Urban or Suburban?

Are you looking to live in the city, or do you prefer the suburbs? Deciding between urban and suburban can be as difficult as choosing between a house and condo.

Living in the city has its benefits. You're closer to where all the action is. Usually, plenty of restaurants, shops and entertainment venues are nearby. You'll save money and time on transportation if you're within walking distance of work. You may not even need a car.

Urban living isn't without its drawbacks. Since you're buying in a prime location, you'll typically pay *more* for *less*. In an urban area, you may only be able to afford a condo. Some people are suited for the condo lifestyle. If you're used to living in a house, it might be a tough adjustment.

In the suburbs, you can typically stretch your home-buying dollar further. If you're planning to raise kids, a house with a yard may be a priority. You may not have nightlife at your doorstep, but you'll likely have the great outdoors—enjoy parks and outdoor activities.

For some, the biggest downside to the suburbs is the distance from downtown. If you work downtown, your travel time will be longer. You'll also be farther from downtown shopping and entertainment.

Buying Outside the Big City

Much of this book's focus is on buying a home in a big city. That's because homes are less affordable there. Big cities tend to have better job opportunities, but those come at a cost (higher home prices). If you live in a small city or town, where homes are more affordable, and you have a decent job, take advantage of this. If you're really focused, maybe you can pay off your mortgage in three years, like I did.

Love Thy Neighbour

You're going to be spending a lot of time beside your neighbours, so it's a good idea to get to know them at least a bit before buying. A good neighbour can make your time at home pleasant; a bad one can make it a living nightmare. Wouldn't you rather be welcomed to the neighbourhood with a gift basket than with a laundry list of complaints?

Take the time to speak to your potential neighbours *before* buying. You'll want to know if there's any bad blood with the current homeowners. The last thing you want is for your new neighbours to direct that hostility toward you.

Neighbours can also be an invaluable source of information. Since they live near your home, they can tell you about all sorts of things you might not think to ask—everything from break and enters to a flooded basement. Take this opportunity to get to know them and start the relationship off on the right foot.

Working with a Real Estate Agent

You've probably heard the term *house hunting*, but have you heard of *real estate agent hunting*? It's a term I use to describe the process of finding the right agent.* Home buying can be competitive. Choosing the right agent can mean the difference between buying your dream home and being left on the sidelines.

The sad reality is that some people spend more time choosing their hairdresser than their agent. When you're buying a home, you may have to make snap decisions that will shape your financial future for years to come. A good agent gives you the knowledge and tools you need to make informed decisions.

Finding the right agent can take time. I was with three agents before finding the right one. My first agent was friendly and helpful, but when it came time to make an offer, she didn't provide me with comparable properties (even after I asked for them), so I had no idea how much to offer and ended up losing out on a nice home. My second agent had the tenacity of a pit bull, but then she just seemed to lose interest. The third time was the charm. My third agent was the perfect fit. He was hands-on, which was great, since I was a first-time home-buyer. He showed me a ton of properties. It took me only a couple of months to find and buy my home.

With so many agents out there, choosing one can feel overwhelming. You might choose the first agent you meet. And you may find the right agent this way, but there's no guarantee. Similar to house hunting, you won't know for sure unless you see what else is out there.

Finding an Agent

Looking for an agent? Here are good places to start:

- **Word of mouth:** Ask for recommendations from family, friends and colleagues who have recently bought a home.

- **Lawn signs:** Look for an agent with lots of lawn signs in the neighbourhood you'd like to buy in. Visit their website to read testimonials.

- **Open houses:** Open houses aren't just for nosy neighbours. They're

---

* There's some confusion surrounding the term *real estate agent*. The brokerage representing you as the buyer is actually the *agent*. More accurate terms are *real estate representative* and *salesperson*. But to keep things simple, I call the latter *agents* throughout the book.

also a great way to meet agents. The agent should already be familiar with your desired neighbourhood.

- **Brokerages:** If there's a real estate brokerage nearby, stop in and mention you're looking for an agent. The brokerage can match you with an agent suited for your home-buying needs.

- **Multiple Listing Service:** Visit the MLS website and search for agents selling homes in your area.

Hiring a Rock-Star Agent

An agent may be a good fit for your friend or colleague, but it doesn't mean you two will be a match made in heaven. Interview at least three agents. Go prepared with a list of questions—this will help you determine whether you're a good match (more on this below). Here are tips for hiring a rock-star agent:

- **Familiarity:** It's important to find an agent who is familiar with the neighbourhood you want to buy in and the types of properties (house, condo, townhouse) you're looking at. You don't want to use an agent familiar only with downtown condos to look at houses in the suburbs.

Use an Agent When Buying a New Home

Don't go it alone when buying a new home. An agent looks after your best interests. They review the agreement and negotiate on your behalf. They can also get you access to some of the best units ahead of the general public.

- **Availability:** The home-buying process can happen at a breakneck pace. You want an agent who will return phone calls and emails in a timely manner if not faster. If your agent is MIA, you could lose out on your dream home. Hopefully the agent will first take the time to see homes in the neighbourhood to find out if they're worth your visiting.

- **A good fit:** You'll want an agent who's not only a good personal fit but a good professional fit. If you're a first-time homebuyer, you'll want an agent who will take the time to walk you through the basics. If you've bought and sold homes before, you might want someone less hands-on but who knows the market like the back of their hand.

• **Agent complaints:** Check with the regulator in the jurisdiction you're buying in (e.g., RECO in Ontario) to make sure no disciplinary action is being taken against the agent.

Four Questions to Ask an Agent Before Signing On

If you're anything like me, you've been to plenty of job interviews. Turn the tables and treat meetings with agents like job interviews— theirs. Sample questions to ask agents include:

1 **How long have you been an active agent?** The word *active* is key—you want an agent who's familiar with the current real estate market. Even if an agent has 20 years' experience, if they've only sold two homes in the last five years, you might think twice before using them.

2 **How many homes have you listed and sold in the last year?** A successful agent should be ready and willing to share this information. If the agent has sold less than four homes, this should raise a red flag.

3 **Will I be working directly with you?** If you're working with a team, find out whether you'll be working with the team lead or a more junior agent.

4 **May I have three references?** A successful agent should have no problem having you contact satisfied buyers and sellers about them. Ask for three of the most recent closes and speak to those people directly.

Review the answers of agents in the comfort of your own home before making your final decision.

Should You Go Exclusive?
The Buyer Agency Agreement

The buyer agency agreement is a legal document that outlines the relationship with the brokerage. (In Ontario, it's the BRA, for "buyer representation agreement," which may be a funny acronym, but don't let it fool you—it's an important legal document.) It includes information such as your desired property type, location, commission and the amount of time of the agreement. It also places fiduciary duty on the brokerage to promote and protect your best interests.

Being an agent can be tough. When your agent helps you look for a home, they won't get paid unless you buy a home with them. The BRA at least guarantees you won't go behind your agent's back and use another agent.

Should you sign a buyer agency agreement? In my experience, it's usually the newer agents who ask you to sign one. When you do, you're committed to working exclusively with the real estate brokerage for the length of the agreement. If your agent is a rock star, it shouldn't be a problem. But what if they're not a good fit? Unless they let you end the agreement early, you're stuck working with the same brokerage until the agreement expires. If you buy a home with an agent at another brokerage, your first agent could sue both the second agent and you for breaching the agreement.

When you're asked to sign a buyer agency agreement, think of yourself like the franchise player on an NBA team. Would Kyle Lowry or LeBron James sign the first contract offer put in front of them? I don't think so. Take time to think it over. If you do decide to sign an agreement, give your agent a trial run. Start with 30 days and see how it goes (signing any longer than three months is nuts!). You can extend it once your agent proves they're a rock star. Also, make sure the agreement is limited to a specific geographic area and property type (e.g., houses, townhouses, or condos).

Check with the regulator in the jurisdiction you're buying in for the rules on buyer agency.

• • • • •

5 Key Mortgage-Burning Takeaways

➤ **Decide between renting and buying.** If your job situation is unstable or you're planning to move in less than five years, you're probably better off renting. If you're in it for the long haul, buying is usually the way to go.

➤ **Choose a house, townhouse or condo.** If you're raising a family, a house can be ideal, since it usually comes with a yard. If you're looking for something low maintenance and don't mind the condo lifestyle, a condo may be your best bet. A townhouse is a good compromise.

➤ **Remember: location, location, location.** You can have the nicest home on the block, but the one thing you can't change is the location. Choose a home in a decent neighbourhood you'll be proud to call home.

➤ **Pick an urban or suburban lifestyle.** Determine where you'd like to live. If you prefer the downtown nightlife, be prepared to pay for it. Your home-buying dollars will generally go further in the suburbs—just be sure you don't mind the longer commute.

➤ **Select a rock-star agent.** A good agent can make your home-buying experience go a lot more smoothly than it might otherwise. Do your research ahead of time, interview at least three agents and choose an agent best suited for your needs.

If you haven't found it yet, keep looking. Don't settle.
As with all matters of the heart, you'll know when you find it.
STEVE JOBS, co-founder of Apple

9

House Rich, Cash Rich
Buying a Dream Home
You Can Afford

YOU'VE MADE SOME tough decisions so far. You've crunched the numbers and decided home buying is the right move for you. You've chosen between a house, townhouse and condo in the suburbs or city. The only thing left is to buy your dream home at a price you can afford.

A common mistake homebuyers make is buying too much home. I'll explain how to avoid this, so you're not house rich, cash poor. Homebuyers today seem to have a wish list longer than a kid does for Santa. I'll help you narrow down your needs and wants to find a home in your budget.

Once you find a home you're interested in, it's time to make an offer. This can be nerve-racking, but it doesn't have to be. I'll tell you what goes on behind the scenes, so you stand a better chance of coming out ahead. Let your home-buying adventure begin!

Finding Your Dream Home

So you want to buy a home, but you're not sure where to look? Start with these good sources:

- **Family and friends:** Tell everyone you know you're looking for a home. You may get the inside scoop on homes coming on the market.

- **Agents:** Finding a home is like a full-time job. Hire an agent who knows the neighbourhood you want to buy in (see chapter 8).

- **Multiple Listing Service:** Visit the MLS website to find homes for sale in your desired neighbourhood.

- **Lawn signs:** Be on the lookout for "for sale" signs in your preferred neighbourhood. This is also a good way to come across homes that are for sale by owner (a topic we'll discuss below).

- **Model homes:** If you're in the market for a preconstruction home, visit model homes in person, to get an idea of what the finished product will look like. To protect your best interests, bring along your agent.

- **Social media:** Follow agents in your desired neighbourhood on Facebook and Twitter. Subscribe to real estate blogs.

Consider "For Sale by Owner" Properties

"For sale by owner" properties tend to not have as many showings as homes sold by agents. Less buyer competition means you have a better chance of purchasing your dream home at an affordable price.

Don't Buy Too Much Home

The simplest way to be mortgage-free sooner is to not take on a massive mortgage. This shouldn't come as a big surprise. The lower your mortgage, the less time it takes to pay off.

Getting pre-approved for a mortgage (more about this in chapter 10) tells you how much home you can afford. Just because the bank says you can spend up to $800,000 on a home doesn't mean you have to. The words *up to* are key here and are what many homebuyers overlook. You don't want to spend so much on a home that it's a drag on your finances.

When I was house hunting, the bank said I could spend up to $500,000. That would mean taking on a mortgage of $330,000 on my own. I didn't feel comfortable with that much debt to my name, so I set myself a maximum purchase price of $450,000. No matter what,

I wouldn't spend more than this amount. In the end, I ended up with my dream home and spent only $425,000. If I had spent $500,000, there's no way I could have paid off my mortgage in three years by age 30. ("Mortgage-free at 33" may have a nicer ring to it, but I'd much rather be mortgage-free at 30.)

When your bank tells you your maximum home purchase price, do the math and see if you're comfortable taking on a mortgage that size. Generally, you don't want to spend more than 37% (42% in pricey real estate markets) of your gross (before tax) monthly income on your monthly mortgage payment, property tax, carrying costs such as heating and other debts (you'll find a detailed example of this in chapter 10). You're almost always better taking on a mortgage *below* the maximum amount you're eligible for. This gives you financial wiggle room if you lose your job or the roof starts to leak.

Let's say that the most you want to spend on a home is $800,000. With a 20% down payment ($160,000), your mortgage will be $640,000. You and your partner can afford to pay $3,500 per month toward the mortgage (you must be lawyers). Write those three figures down on a piece of paper, fold it up and stick it in your wallet *before* heading to the bank. Heck, tattoo it on your forehead if you have to.* When your banker says that you can spend $1 million on your "dream home," stick to your guns. Know that $800,000 is the most you're willing to spend on a home, end of story.

Still Not Convinced?

A common argument for buying as much home as you can is that your principal residence is tax sheltered. Real estate has been on a tear in Canada over the last two decades. Since the family home is one of the last tax-sheltered investments, why wouldn't you buy a McMansion if you can afford it? All your money may be tied up, but if you ever need it, you can tap into your equity with a HELOC. What's not to love? Plenty.

Bigger isn't always better, especially when it comes to home buying. What people seem to forget is that a bigger home comes with higher

---

* Please note this is only a joke. Please do *not* do that! I'm not responsible for the tattoo removal cost if you're foolish enough to listen to me.

carrying costs. You'll shell out more for property tax, heating and electricity. You're not going to want to leave those extra rooms empty, so you'll spend more on furniture. With your cash flow tied up, you're not able to save for other long-term goals like retirement. Not to mention, you're not properly diversified, since all your money is tied up in your home. (*Diversification* is a way to reduce risk by choosing different types of investments, for example bonds, GICs and mutual funds.)

Needs vs. Wants (AKA a Jacuzzi Is *Not* a Need)

For most buyers, a home represents the single largest financial transaction of their life. Time taken to come up with a list of needs and wants is time well spent (it takes about the same time as watching an episode of *House of Cards*). Get it right and you'll find a home you'll be proud to call your own for the years to come. Get it wrong and you could find yourself on the move again soon.

Your list of needs and wants gives you laser focus. You'll save time by only looking at homes in your price range. This will help you avoid disappointment and celebrate your mortgage-burning party that much sooner.

Some buyers seem to have their needs and wants mixed up. Things that used to be called luxuries (wants) have become must-haves (needs). My friend Patricia won't step foot inside a home she's considering buying unless it has hardwood floors, granite countertops, and stainless-steel appliances (let's just say she's "high maintenance"). That's fine and dandy if you have six figures in your bank account (not counting cents), but for everyone else, trade-offs likely have to be made.

Coming up with a list of needs and wants can seem daunting, but it doesn't have to be. It's helpful to start with your current digs. What do you like? What do you dislike? You may enjoy being a 10-minute walk from work but despise the cramped kitchen where there isn't enough room to swing a cat (sorry, Grumpy Cat). Next, picture your dream home. How many bedrooms does it have? What neighbourhood is it in? Does it have features like a Jacuzzi and a white picket fence? This will be a good start.

Creating Your List of Needs and Wants

Now the real fun starts. Jot down anything that comes to mind. This is a family decision, so be sure to involve your significant other and kids, if you have any.

Once you have your list, look at each item line by line and figure out if it's a need or a want. For example, you may "need" three bedrooms and want two bathrooms.

Don't fool yourself into thinking a want is really a need. Unless you're a professional tennis player, you probably don't need a tennis court in your backyard.

Next, prioritize your list. Position the most important items at the top. Try to come up with a top-10 list. Here's a list of needs and wants to get you started.

EXAMPLE

NEEDS (THINGS YOU CAN'T LIVE WITHOUT)	WANTS (NICE-TO-HAVES)
1 Three bedrooms	1 Jacuzzi
2 Two bathrooms	2 Deck
3 Safe neighbourhood	3 Remodelled kitchen
4 Good schools	4 Newly renovated bathroom
5 Garage for storage	5 Hardwood floors
6 Parking	6 Newer windows
7 Yard	7 Skylight
8 Near transit	8 Fireplace
9 Home office	9 Sunroom
10 Updated wiring and plumbing	10 Bay window

Once you've come up with your list of needs and wants, share it with your agent. Based on this list, they can help you find a home in your price range. Be prepared to make trade-offs—which is never fun or easy, but a lot simpler when armed with your list.

Stretching Your Home-Buying Dollar Further

Coming up with a list of needs and wants can be a reality check. You may not be able to afford to buy a home in your family neighbourhood right away.

When I started house hunting, my heart was set on a three-bedroom house. The problem was that I couldn't afford it in my desired neighbourhood—I could afford only a two-bedroom house. I made the tough decision of moving farther away, to where I could afford a spacious three-bedroom house. Although it added an extra 20 minutes to my daily commute, I still feel it's worth it. The decision was a lot easier once I made my list of needs and wants.

If you can't afford to buy in your dream neighbourhood, you'll need to look at other options. Moving to the suburbs is one. Or buy in an up-and-coming area: in every city, often-overlooked low-profile neighbourhoods are being transformed and are now proving especially popular with first-time homebuyers.

Is It Wise to Buy a Home You'll Grow Into?

To justify buying a bigger home, a little white lie we often tell ourselves is that we're buying a home we'll grow into. This may be true sometimes, but it's often just an excuse to buy a home we can't afford.

Think long and hard before deciding on the size of your home. If you have a child on the way, you'll likely want to buy a home with enough bedrooms, but if you're only thinking of starting a family "one day," it may not make sense to buy a home with an extra bedroom or two for a family that may never exist.

A bigger home comes with more expenses. Try to buy a home that will suit your needs for at least the next five years. You can always upsize when you're ready (although, as mentioned, you don't want to move too often, as each time you'll pay closing costs—something we discuss in chapter 12).

New vs. Resale

Is your dream home brand-new or resale? It's a personal decision for many. Growing up, my family always lived in resale homes; I couldn't imagine living in a new home. I ended up buying a 1950s bungalow. But that's just me. You may have grown up in a new home and prefer those.

Not sure whether to buy new or resale? Consider the following pros and cons.

New Homes

Pros

- **Customizable:** You have a lot more choice. Sometimes you can choose everything down to the kitchen sink. If you've always dreamed of marble countertops and hardwood floors, there's nothing stopping you from getting them (provided you have the money).

- **Contemporary style:** Enjoy the latest trends, like a fireplace in the master bathroom.

- **Turnkey:** New homes usually come with lower maintenance and repair costs, since everything is brand spanking new.

- **Energy efficient:** New homes tend to be energy efficient, meaning relatively low utility bills. New homes are usually more environmentally friendly, lowering your carbon footprint.

- **Protection:** New homes are built according to the latest building codes and standards. If you run into problems, you're often covered by a home warranty.

Cons

- **Builder delays:** Don't get too attached to your move-in date. It's not uncommon for builder delays to push it later.

- **Heftier down payment:** You'll usually fork over a heftier down payment. On a resale home, the down payment can be as little as 5%, but on a new home, you often have to put down 20%. As such, you might not be able to afford a new home in pricey real estate markets.

- **Not always as advertised:** A finished home may look different from what you had imagined. The square footage may come in less than advertised (external walls and balconies are sometimes included in the measurements).

- **Conflict of interest:** You're buying directly from the builder and its hired sales agents, so you don't get the same objective advice you would from an independent real estate agent.

- **Hidden costs:** New homes have plenty of hidden surprises. You may have to fork over more money for everything from paving the driveway to landscaping. Review the sales agreement carefully to see what's covered.

- **New neighbourhood:** At first, there may not be much to see and do. It could take months or even years until amenities like shopping malls and movie theatres are built nearby.

- **Limited design choices:** New homes tend to offer cookie-cutter layouts and designs. They don't have the same character as a resale home.

Resale Homes

Pros
- **Charm and character:** Like fine wine, houses tend to get better with age. It's hard to beat the charm and character of an older house.

- **More choice:** Choose from a variety of home types (bungalow, two-storey, duplex, and so on) in neighbourhoods across the city.

- **Established neighbourhood:** There are usually plenty of amenities nearby to enjoy.

- **Extras:** You usually don't have to worry about landscaping or fencing, since it's typically already taken care of.

- **Negotiating power:** In buyers' and balanced markets, the list price is often more negotiable than with new homes. If you're lucky, you may even get the seller to throw in extras like garden tools.

Cons
- **Higher upkeep costs:** Since the home is older, be prepared to spend more on maintenance and repairs.

- **Costly renovations:** Everything from the appliances to the roof may need to be replaced or upgraded in the not-too-distant future.

- **Higher utility costs:** Older homes tend to be less energy efficient than new homes, meaning relatively high utility bills.

- **Dated design:** Some people call it charm and character, other people call it old and worn out. Although you can renovate your home to modernize it, that costs money you may not have.

Is a Fixer Upper Worth It?

A fixer upper can be a great way to buy a home in a good neighbourhood at an affordable price. It can be a handyperson's dream—or a homeowner's worst nightmare. It usually comes with plenty of surprises, not always good.

If you've ever watched *Income Property*, you'll know what I'm talking about. A home may look fine on the surface, then you start tearing down the walls and find not-so-pleasant surprises—like mould or rotting beams. This can make your home renovation budget skyrocket.

Me, I decided against a fixer upper. I'm the first to admit I'm no Mike Holmes. Although I can handle simple renovations like painting, that's about as far as my skills go. I wanted a home with a basement apartment I could rent out from day one.

Still on the fence? Consider some key points. First, don't bite off more than you can chew. Look for a home with mostly cosmetic touch-ups. This can be as easy as slapping on a new coat of paint. Structural repairs are often a lot more complicated—and costly. If there are foundation problems, it might be best to run for the hills.

Second, if you're planning a DIY renovation, do you have the time? Working 70 to 80 hours a week, I simply didn't have the time for renos. If you do have the time, expertise and desire to do home renovations, then by all means go ahead. Just remember, renovations don't happen in the blink of the eye, as home renovation shows would have you believe.

And finally, do your homework. If you know a home needs repairs, take the time to find out how costly they will be before making an offer. When I was looking at a home with a tilting chimney, I had a contractor take a look and provide me with an estimate.

Five Ways to Pay for Home Renos

You may buy a fixer upper at a bargain-basement price, but you could end up spending a pretty penny on renos. Consider these five ways to pay for home renos:

1 If you have the money, you can use your own savings.

2 You can lower your down payment, financing your renos with a larger mortgage.

3 You can get a purchase plus improvements mortgage. Add to your mortgage up to the *lesser* of 10% of the purchase price or $40,000 for improvements that add value to the property. The additional cost is "added" to the purchase price. For example, if you buy a home for $450,000, the minimum 5% down payment is $22,500. Add $40,000 in approved renos and the new purchase price in the eyes of the bank is $490,000; the minimum 5% down payment bumps to $24,500. This is a great option, one that doesn't get the attention it deserves.

4 If you have a down payment of 20% or more, you are eligible for a HELOC. Getting one makes sense if you're doing improvements down the road, or if the renos may take a long time and are being done in stages (you pay interest only on the money withdrawn, but it comes at a higher rate than your mortgage).

5 You can use a personal line of credit. This typically comes with fairly high interest rates but is a good option if your reno budget isn't huge and you plan on paying the debt down quickly.

Five Tips for Hiring an Expert Contractor

Hiring a contractor can be nerve-racking, since the home renovation industry is largely unregulated. You really have to do your homework.

I have had my fair share of experience with contractors. One morning I woke up to find two inches of water in my basement kitchen. The retaining wall had shifted, causing water to flood underneath the exterior basement door. I knew this was too big a project to handle myself, so I started phoning around for estimates.

Most contractors are honest, but the few bad apples have given the industry a bad rap. Here are five tips for hiring an expert contractor.

1. Shop Around

When it comes to TVs and laptops, we're more than happy to shop around, so why do some homeowners not do the same for contractors? When you're spending thousands of dollars on renos, be sure to take the time to get quotes from at least three contractors. Where the heck do you find contractors? Word of mouth, referrals from family and friends, lawn signs and websites like HomeStars are good places to start.

2. The Lowest Quote Isn't Always the Best

It can be tempting to accept the lowest quote, but it isn't always the wisest decision. A quote that comes in a lot lower than the others is often a red flag. A low quote could mean the contractor will cut corners or doesn't know what he's doing. I got several quotes on my retaining wall; one was only $3,500, whereas another was a whopping $18,000. I ended up choosing a quote somewhere in the middle.

3. Do Your Research

After reviewing several quotes, make a shortlist of two to three contractors. Before making a final decision, do your research. Check on the Better Business Bureau website for complaints. Also visit Home-Stars to read reviews from customers. Ask for references, and take the time to phone them. If possible, visit properties with recently completed renovations similar to yours.

Have a Contingency Fund

When doing a reno, be prepared for the unexpected—like asbestos. Set aside a contingency fund of at least 10% of the project's budget.

4. Get Your Quote in Writing

Don't be shy to ask for the quote in writing. A written quote is a must—it spells out everything covered under the project, to avoid any misunderstanding. If something in the contract is unclear, don't be shy to query it. If the contractor gives you a hard time, go with someone else.

5. Don't Pay Too Much Up Front

Never give more than a 50% deposit up front, and try to give less than that. (Some contractors ask for no money down since they can always put a lien on your house for unpaid debt.) Even honest contractors can run into financial difficulties; you don't want your contractor to file for bankruptcy before the work has even started. To stay in control, pay your contractor in instalments.

Buying a Home with a Secondary Suite

If you're interested in a rental property, buying a house with a basement apartment is a good starting point. A secondary suite usually doesn't take as much time and energy to manage as a standalone rental property. You'll also be able to keep a closer eye on the property, since you're living there.

A basement apartment can be a good way to subsidize your mortgage. Instead of using your basement for storage, why not use it to generate income and pay off your mortgage in half the time? Let's say you rent out your basement suite for $800 per month. Over 25 years (the maximum length of high-ratio mortgages), that's $240,000 in rent (and that's assuming you don't raise the rent). That's a lot of dough!

If your home already has a basement apartment, there's nothing stopping you from sprucing it up with a fresh coat of paint and putting it up for rent tomorrow. If you own a home with a partially finished basement and a separate exterior entrance, consider adding a kitchen and bathroom to turn it into a secondary suite. These renovations can pay for themselves. Not only do you get a steady stream of rental income, but it can boost the resale value of your home. This is only the tip of the iceberg on secondary suites. We'll explore being a landlord in more detail in chapter 14.

Important things to consider when house hunting for a property with a secondary suite include:

- **Is the secondary suite in good shape?** If only a few cosmetic upgrades are needed but otherwise it is in good shape, you can put it up for rent easily.

- **Is the rental unit legal?** In some cities and towns, it's illegal to rent out a secondary suite. Even if it's legal, find out if the suite complies with fire and electrical codes, property bylaws and residential zoning requirements, among other things, *before* you buy.

- **Does it have a separate exterior entrance?** Installing an entrance is expensive. Look for a home that already has one.

- **How tall is the ceiling?** Many municipalities require a ceiling height of at least seven feet (just over two metres) for a secondary suite to be considered legal.

- **Is it in a desirable location?** Look in a location tenants will want to rent. Try to find a home close to schools, shopping and transit.

- **Is there parking?** If there isn't parking space for the tenant, it may be more difficult to rent the suite.

- **Does it have laundry?** People don't want to haul their dirty clothes to the laundromat. If there isn't space for shared laundry, consider putting in a stackable washer and dryer.

Consider Other Costs

Homeownership comes with more costs than just the purchase price. Here are the three major ones:

Appealing Your Property Assessment
To better your chances of successfully appealing your property assessment, include data for comparable properties, along with any reasons your home may be overvalued (e.g., you're close to a busy main street or apartment buildings; see Signs of a Poor Location).

- **Home insurance:** Home insurance protects your home and its contents. Your premium depends on several factors, including the home's value and age, and the deductible. Most lenders require that you have home insurance before they'll approve your mortgage. You'll find more details on this in chapter 13.

- **Property tax:** Property tax is a major expense for homeowners. Before buying a home, find out how much your property tax bill will be. Property tax is based on the assessed value of the home. If your property tax seems too high, consider filing an appeal. The process for filing an appeal is different, depending on where you live. There's often a deadline to file your appeal. Visit your province's property assessment website (e.g., MPAC for Ontario) for more details.

- **Closing costs:** Closing costs are referred to as the *transactional cost* of real estate and are often overlooked by homebuyers. They're anything but a drop in the bucket, typically adding up to between 1.5% and 4% of a home's purchase price. Common closing costs are a home inspection, real estate lawyer fees, land transfer tax and appraisal fees, among others. Closing costs are covered in more depth in chapter 12.

What to Look for at Showings and Open Houses

You've see the listing for a home and you like what you see. You're ready to take the next step and visit the home in person to see if it lives up to the hype. You have two options: set up a showing or visit an open house. A *showing* is when your agent books an appointment for a private viewing of the property, usually lasting for 30 to 60 minutes. With an *open house*, the home is open for anyone to come in and see without an appointment. Open houses usually take place on Saturday and Sunday afternoon during a set time, like 2 p.m. to 4 p.m.

To make sure a home's looking its best, selling agents advise sellers on things to do to boost their home's appeal, including staging, painting and landscaping. Sometimes sellers try to distract buyers from needed costly repairs with what handyman Mike Holmes calls "lipstick and mascara." Try to look beyond cosmetic updates like new doorknobs and refaced kitchen cabinets. Treat your viewing like a home inspection. Pay special attention to the "bones" of the home. Make sure the roof is in good shape, the windows and plumbing are upgraded, and the furnace is relatively new. You'll probably see plenty of homes, so take good notes. It's easy to forget things and to mix up the homes in your mind. Write down your likes and dislikes about each property.

Be on the lookout for red flags. For example, when I viewed a house near a ravine, I noticed there was mould in the basement. When I asked the agent about it, he mentioned the home had some "damp-ness issues." Scented candles are another red flag. Although they may produce a wonderful aroma, the seller could be trying to use them to mask a not-so-pleasant odour.

Even if you do take a close look at the home during the showing, it's still wise to get a home inspection. But by paying attention during the showing, you can save time and money. If you don't like what you see, you won't waste your time making an offer and paying for a home inspection.

A Winning Offer to Purchase

Buying a home is a lot like dating. No, seriously, hear me out. You spend a lot of time searching for your soulmate (your dream home). For some, looks (cosmetics) matter just as much as personality (the plumbing, electrical, furnace and so on). You can search for your per-fect match on dating (real estate listing) websites or go speed dating (to open houses). Once you find someone you're interested in (a home that meets your needs), you go out on a first date (a showing). If you like what you see and you have a good time, you try to seal the deal with a kiss (by making an offer to purchase). You plant one on the lips (your offer is accepted), or you get the cheek (you're rejected).

The offer includes important information, including buyer and seller information, offer price, deposit amount, walk-throughs of the property (usually three), conditions, chattels, fixtures, closing date and expiration date (how long the seller has to accept the offer).

This section mostly focuses on resale homes. If you're buying a new home, you'll negotiate directly with the builder, so you won't have to deal with the headache of a bidding war. That being said, it still helps to look at comparable properties to see if you're getting a good deal.

When you're buying resale, you won't pay GST/HST on the pur-chase price (though you'll pay it on other closing costs, like your lawyer's fees and some disbursements). If you're buying a new home, don't forget to budget for GST/HST (though you may qualify for the GST/HST new housing rebate). Ask the builder if the purchase price already includes GST/HST.

Conditional Offer or Clean Offer?

You've found your dream home and you're ready to make an offer. Not so fast. You'll have to decide the type of offer to make: conditional or clean.

A *clean offer* is one that's free and clear of conditions. When the seller signs off, it's a done deal. A *conditional offer*, on the other hand, has at least one condition that must be satisfied for the deal to go through. You can include conditions for just about anything, though the most common are financing, home inspection and broom-swept and, for a condo, a status certificate review (the status certificate includes important details about your condo, such as the reserve fund, any special assessments or lawsuits, condo bylaws, rules, mainte-nance fees and utilities; ask your lawyer to review it.) Although they're not conditions per se, ask for three walk-throughs as well.

Conditions exist to protect buyers. If your bank doesn't approve your mortgage or you find during the inspection that the house has termites, you may be able to get out of the deal.

What type of offer should you make? This depends on your finan-cial situation and the type of market you're buying in. In a seller's market, you'll put yourself at a distinct disadvantage by having too many conditions, especially during bidding wars.

Conditions Can Cost You Money—and Your Dream Home

I wish I had had a better understanding of conditions when I first started house hunting. Even though I was pre-approved for a mort-gage, I included a condition of financing in my first two offers. Big mistake! I ended up losing out on both houses. I actually outbid one buyer by over $5,000, but because his offer was clean and mine wasn't, the seller chose his offer.

As the proverb goes, "A bird in the hand is worth two in the bush." Sellers may be willing to accept a clean offer at a slightly lower offer price over a conditional offer at a higher offer price. They'd rather have a sure thing than worry about a conditional offer hitting a snag.

Think long and hard before including conditions, as they could cost you your dream home. If you do include conditions, make the deadlines tight—two or three days for a home inspection and a week for financing are generally enough.

Conditions Done the Right Way

Don't include conditions in your offer just for the sake of including conditions—include only those you truly need. Buyers in seller's markets are often skipping home inspections in bidding wars. I wouldn't advise skipping your home inspection (inspections often turn up costly needed repairs, like on the furnace, foundation or roof), but if you're in a bidding war and want to present a clean offer, there's always the option of getting a pre-inspection. A regular home inspection takes place *after* your offer is accepted, whereas a pre-inspection happens *before* your offer. Both inspections are essentially the same; only the timing differs. This may give you a leg up on the competition. (Although there's no guarantee the seller will accept your offer, which means you could be out some $500 or more for a home inspection. Ouch!)

Likewise, if you're pre-approved for a mortgage, consider leaving out the condition of financing.

Chattels and Fixtures

Don't forget about chattels and fixtures—they've caused disagreements among buyers and sellers on countless occasions. It's not always clear what's a chattel and what's a fixture. *Chattels* are generally movable objects like the stove and fridge, a wall-hung TV, mirrors and drapery, whereas *fixtures* are attached to the home and not easily moved—a built-in dishwasher, range hood, light fixtures and faucets, for instance.

Chattels are usually included in the listing, but there's nothing stopping you from asking for more (I asked for—and got—the seller's garden tools, which saved me at least $300 by not having to go out and buy them myself). To be on the safe side, list all chattels and existing light fixtures in your offer (sellers have been known to swap out beautiful chandeliers with cheap light fixtures before moving out). If you want to go a step further, take photos and list the makes and models. There's no such thing as too much detail.

Deciding on an Offer Price

The offer price is the most important part of your offer. The seller and you are at odds. You want to buy the home for the lowest price possible, the seller wants to sell the home for top dollar. There will be some give and take. When making the offer, you'll have three choices:

1 Offer **less** than the list price.
2 Offer the **list price.**
3 Offer **more** than the list price.

You don't want to just pull your offer price out of a hat. Look at comparable properties, the seller's motivation and how many buyers you're up against.

Look at Comparable Properties

It's hard to know if a home is reasonably priced without looking at what else is out there. Just as you'd comparison shop for a new laptop, comparison shop for your home. Your agent can lend you a helping hand.

Comparable properties (or "comps," as the kids say) are similar homes in the same or nearby neighbourhoods. Comps can be both homes currently for sale and those that have sold recently. When deciding on an offer price, look at homes sold in the last six months. Your agent should be able to provide you with similar homes on the market and those that have recently sold.

It's useful to know what you're going up against. For example, if you're interested only in a specific type of home—a three-bedroom bungalow in a specific neighbourhood, say—it could mean you're up against stiff competition from other interested buyers if it's the only property of its kind available in the neighbourhood.

For homes that have recently sold, pay attention to sold price, not listing price. For homes currently on the market, find out how many days the home has been on the market (referred to as "days on market"). If it has been on the market for a while or the seller has reduced the price, you may have more room to negotiate.

Why Is the Seller's Home on the Market?

As the buyer, it helps to know why the seller is selling. Common reasons to sell a home include divorce, downsizing, moving up, relocating for a job and a death in the family. Do your own investigation. If you know the seller's motivation, you may be able to use it to your advantage. Casually ask the seller's agent why the home is for sale. The agent may willingly divulge details. Before I made an offer on my home, I learned that the seller had already moved out of the province and was anxious to sell off what he had left behind. Based on this, I made a fair offer—and ended up buying my dream home.

A little kindness can go a long way. Sellers are human beings too. I've heard of buyers delivering freshly baked cookies. I even read about a couple who had been looking for a home for months, with no luck—they always ended up in a bidding war. So they decided to make a personal postcard plea, which helped them eventually buy their dream home.

Sealing the Deal

By now you have a good idea of how to determine how much to offer for a property. Now it's time to put pen to paper and make it official. Go prepared with a deposit in the form of a certified cheque or bank draft payable to the seller's real estate brokerage in trust, in case your offer is accepted. (Whatever you do, don't write a cheque to the seller; if the seller blows your money or goes bankrupt, your deposit could be as good as gone.)

If you're the only buyer making an offer, you'll have a lot more leeway. You may wish to start with a lower offer price with conditions. If you're up against other buyers and you really want the home, you'll want to come in with the best offer you can afford (and ideally a clean offer). Don't assume the seller will counteroffer. If you hold back your best offer and another buyer makes a better offer, you can kiss your dream home goodbye (more on bidding wars below).

Don't just blindly sign the offer. It represents a legal document for quite possibly the single biggest purchase of your lifetime. Although most agents use standard offer forms, it's the extras like chattels that can get missed. Take time to review the offer and make sure everything is included. If it's not in writing, it's not official.

Deposit: Getting Some Skin in the Game

Buying a home is a major purchase. You're expected to make a deposit when making an offer, in order to show that you're serious. Your deposit is usually paid by a certified cheque or bank draft to the seller's real estate brokerage and held in trust.

There's no hard-and-fast rule about deposit size. It depends on where and the type of property you're buying. If you're buying a resale home in a big city where the real estate market is very competitive, be prepared to cough up more. Your deposit is typically anywhere from a few hundred dollars to 5% of the purchase price. Your agent comes in handy here; they should know the market well. Ask them how much of a deposit to make.

If you're buying a new home, the deposit structure is slightly different. It's typically broken down into smaller instalments. For example, you may pay $5,000 with your offer, 5% at 30 days, 5% at 90 days, 5% at 180 days and 5% at occupancy (this is pretty standard, although it can vary slightly from project to project). For projects closer to completion, you may be able to negotiate a more lenient deposit structure with the builder.

Stagger Your Deposit

If you don't have the cash on hand to make a 5% deposit when buying resale, stagger the deposit. Make one deposit at the time of offer (as much as you can afford) and a second deposit once any conditions have cleared.

Surviving a Bidding War

In red-hot real estate markets, bidding wars are a fact of life. They're good for sellers, not so good for buyers. Bidding wars can drive the price of a home you're interested in into the stratosphere. Some sellers purposely list their property low to encourage a frenzied bidding war. Recently, the sale of a house in Toronto erupted into a 25-person bidding war—it sold for $717,336, almost $170,000 over asking price![1] This is just one of many examples.

If you find your dream home, chances are you're not alone. Just like a first date, you shouldn't fall in love (at least, that's what my mother says). Don't get caught up in the heat of the moment and go over your budget.

Some buyers, often foreign buyers, can afford to go $200,000 or more over asking because they're paying in cash. If you're taking out a mortgage from the bank, you don't have that same luxury. It's best to walk away.

Coming up on the losing end of a bidding war is never fun. My best advice is to learn to let go. There'll always be other homes. Stay positive and remain patient. You'll come up on the winning end eventually.

Making a Bully Offer

A common strategy of selling agents in red-hot housing markets is to hold back offers. Here's how it typically works: The selling agent brings out a new listing on a weekday—a Wednesday, say—usually at a below-market list price, blitzes it for a week, not accepting offers until the following Wednesday (the *holdback date*). Since many buyers get to see the property, there's a greater chance of a bidding war.

As a buyer, you can fight back by making a bully offer. When you make a bully offer, you don't wait for the holdback date—you make your offer right away, often above list price. If this happens, the selling agent must call the agents of any other interested buyers, to give them the chance to make offers.

On the house I ended up buying, the seller was holding back offers, so I threw caution to the wind and made a *bully offer* over asking. The only condition I included was home inspection, and I made a tight deadline of only two days. This strategy worked perfectly: I bought my dream home at a reasonable price without a bidding war.

A bully offer is a gamble that may or may not pay off. It worked for me, but it might not work for you. Discuss it with your agent before making this type of offer.

● ● ● ● ●

5 Key Mortgage-Burning Takeaways

➤ **Find your dream home.** Your agent is a great resource but shouldn't be your only source. Family, friends, the MLS website, lawn signs, open houses and social media are all potential sources.

➤ **Weigh your needs and wants.** To narrow down your home search, make a list of needs and wants. Work with your agent to find homes in your price range that meet most of your needs and some of your wants.

➤ **Decide whether to buy new or resale.** New homes offer contemporary styles and are customizable. Resale homes come with charm and character in already established neighbourhoods.

➤ **Do your homework on fixer uppers.** Fixer uppers can a good way to afford a home in your dream neighbourhood. Before making an offer, figure out how much the renos will cost you and how you will pay for them.

➤ **Make a winning offer.** Ask your agent for details of comparable properties. Find out the seller's motivation. When you're in a bidding war, make your best offer first (preferably a clean offer).

*Paying off your home early lowers your risk
and gives you security. No math in the world can give you that.*
DAVE RAMSEY, bestselling author and radio host

10

The Ins and Outs
of Mortgages
Everything You Need to Know

YOU'VE FOUND A home you like. You're ready to make an offer. You're almost at the finish line. The only thing standing between you and sweet, sweet victory is a little thing called a mortgage.

A mortgage is the loan that helps you buy your home. It is quite possibly the single biggest financial commitment you'll ever make (no pressure), so you'll want to get it right. Your local bank branch is a good *first* stop when shopping for a mortgage, but it shouldn't be your *only* stop.

In this chapter you'll learn everything you need to know so you can make a well-informed decision when it comes time to sign on the dotted line.

Qualifying for a Mortgage

Have you ever wondered how your bank determines the mortgage amount homebuyers qualify for? It doesn't just toss a coin (although, given some of the NINJA—short for "no income no job or assets"—mortgages the U.S. banks were approving leading up to the 2007–2009 subprime mortgage crisis, maybe they were).

Understanding the mortgage qualification process is like knowing the trick to coming out ahead in Las Vegas (hint: the house always wins). You're more likely to end up in your dream home when you know the rules of the game. Qualifying for a mortgage answers the all-important question, how much house can I afford? Lenders use four mortgage qualification factors.

Factor 1: Income

A mortgage is a lot of money, so it shouldn't come as a surprise that lenders are looking for people with stable income. If you're between jobs, working on contract, self-employed or scalping baseball tickets for a living, you may have a tough time qualifying for a mortgage.

Qualifying for a mortgage is also a lot easier when you're not flying solo. Your co-buyer doesn't have to be your romantic partner—it can be your mother, father, aunt, uncle, adult child, another relative or a friend. By combining your yearly income with someone else's, you can qualify for that much more house. This is helpful in pricey real estate markets; just don't use it as an excuse to buy a home you can't afford. All things considered equal, the bigger the paycheque you take home, the bigger the mortgage you'll qualify for.

Factor 2: Down Payment

Your down payment is another area where size matters. The bigger your down payment, the bigger the mortgage you qualify for (again, all things considered equal). In a perfect world, there'd be world peace, Starbucks coffees would cost a dime and everyone would have a down payment over 20%. Unfortunately, the world is far from perfect.

If you have a down payment of 20% or more, you'll qualify for something called a conventional mortgage. Don't let the financial lingo fool you—it's just a fancy way to say you won't have to pay mortgage insurance. For those with a down payment of less than 20%, your mortgage is considered high ratio. You'll have to bite the bullet and get mortgage insurance.

Factor 3: Debt Ratios

Besides your income and down payment, lenders care about your personal debt. This makes perfect sense—if most of your monthly cash flow is tied up with debt like an auto loan and a line of credit, it leaves you less of a cushion if you run into a financial emergency. Ideally, you'll have no personal debt when applying for a mortgage. (If you have credit card debt costing you 18% or more, focus on paying that off first.) There are two debt ratios lenders use for qualifying home-buyers: gross debt service ratio and total debt service ratio.

Gross Debt Service Ratio

The *gross debt service (GDS) ratio* looks at the portion of your gross monthly income needed to cover your monthly housing costs (e.g., mortgage payment, property tax, heating and 50% of maintenance fees). Most lenders in Canada are looking for a ratio of 35% or below, although if you have a credit score over 680, some lenders let you go as high as 39%. To avoid being house rich, cash poor, aim for a GDS ratio 30% or below (up to 35% in pricey real estate markets).

EXAMPLE GDS RATIO

Let's say funnyman Will Ferrell decides to take a break from Hollywood. He takes a big pay cut to work as a news anchor in Calgary (he was in the movie *Anchorman*... maybe he's doing some method acting?). He loves the newsroom, so he decides to buy a house. Let's see if he'll get approved.

$$\text{GDS ratio} = \frac{\$1,\!418 \text{ (mortgage)} + \$240 \text{ (property tax)} + \$100 \text{ (heating)}}{\$6,\!500 \text{ (gross monthly income)}}$$
$$= 27.05\%$$

Will's GDS ratio is below 35%, so he's passed the first debt-ratio hurdle. Phew!

Total Debt Service Ratio

The *total debt service (TDS) ratio* takes the gross debt service ratio a step further. It looks at the portion of your gross monthly income needed to cover your monthly housing costs, plus monthly debt payments (e.g., car loan, credit card debt, line of credit, student loan). Most lenders in Canada are looking for a ratio of 42% or below, although if you have a credit score over 680, some lenders let you go as high as 44%. Aim for a TDS ratio of 37% or below (up to 42% in high-cost cities).

EXAMPLE TDS RATIO

Continuing on with the example above, Will Ferrell loves Calgary so much, he goes out and buys a car on his lunch break. Let's see if he'll pass the second debt ratio.

$$\text{TDS ratio} = \frac{\$1{,}418\,(\text{mortgage}) + \$240\,(\text{property tax}) + \$100\,(\text{heating}) + \$350\,(\text{car loan})}{\$6{,}500\,(\text{gross monthly income})}$$
$$= 32.43\%$$

Ferrell's TDS ratio is below 42%, so he's passed the second debt-ratio hurdle with flying colours. Ron Burgundy would be proud! (Let's just hope he's wearing pants.)

Focus on Paying Off Unsecured Debt

In the TDS ratio, 3% of the outstanding balance of unsecured debt with a non-fixed payment (e.g., credit cards and unsecured lines of credit) is used. So $10,000 in credit card debt represents a $300 liability, even if the minimum payment is only $150. By buckling down and paying off your credit card balance, on a 25-year mortgage at 2.99%, you'd qualify for $60,000 more in mortgage (provided your GDS ratio is not already at or over the limit).

Why Debt Ratios Matter

Just because the bank lets you have a TDS ratio as high as 44% doesn't mean yours should be that high. I'm going to let you in on a secret: there's a serious flaw in the bank's debt-ratio calculations. All that debt ratios look at is whether your gross monthly income is enough to cover your mortgage, property tax, heating and other debts. The ratios fail to consider everyday expenses such as groceries, transportation, daycare, home maintenance and repairs, to name a few. A lower GDS ratio gives you breathing room if your mortgage rate goes up upon renewal or you lose your job, since your mortgage payments will be more affordable.

A high debt ratio is a clear indication you're buying a home out of your price range, you have a lot of personal debt—or both. If you're buying in pricey markets like Toronto and Vancouver, your debt service ratios will be higher. In cities like those, renting out a portion of your home is a good way to be mortgage-free sooner.

Move Over, There's a New Debt Ratio in Town

Rob Carrick, personal finance columnist with the *Globe and Mail*, came up with his own debt ratio, the *total debt service + savings (TDSS) ratio*. Whereas the TDS ratio looks at your ability to repay your mortgage and other debts, the TDSS ratio looks at your ability to handle all your debts and save 10% of your paycheque. The TDSS ratio is what people should really be paying attention to. Carrick recommends having a TDSS ratio under 40% (up to 50% in pricey markets). Use the extra cash cushion to your benefit—pay down your mortgage sooner.

Factor 4: Credit Score

Unless you're filthy rich and you can afford to buy your home in cash (can you adopt me?), maintaining a good credit score is important. Not only does your credit score help you qualify for a mortgage, it can help you obtain the best mortgage rate, saving you thousands of dollars in interest over the life of your mortgage. If your credit score isn't the greatest, you could pay a higher mortgage rate, or your application could be denied altogether. Not only does a poor credit score make it harder to borrow money, you could have a tough time finding a rental unit, since landlords often look at credit.

Credit has three parts: credit history, credit report and credit score. Your *credit history* is a lot like your resumé. It's a summary of any time you've borrowed money. From your car loan to that $1,000 cell-phone bill you'd like to forget, your credit history is a tell-all of any time you've been extended credit. Your *credit report* is like an annual performance review of your credit history. This is where the student loan you failed to pay back in college can come back to haunt you.

Last but not least is your *credit score*. Your credit score is the magic number that lenders care so much about. You credit score is based on your credit history. This number helps lenders decide whether to approve your mortgage. The higher your credit score, the more favourable the mortgage terms will be. Credit scores typically fall somewhere between 300 and 900.

Credit scores don't just come out of thin air. Credit reporting agencies keep track of your credit history and credit score. You can obtain a copy of your credit report for free, so take advantage of it. The easiest and fastest way is to use Equifax and TransUnion's interactive phone services. You can also download and complete forms from the Equifax and TransUnion websites. You used to have to pay for your credit score, but you can now get it for free online from fintech (financial technology) companies like Borrowell and Mogo. Best of all, it won't lower your credit score to check. Request a copy of your credit report and find out what your credit score is at least a year ahead of when you're thinking of buying a home, to avoid any nasty surprises. (If your credit score is poor, you need time to work on improving it. This can take a year or more because of reporting lags.) If you find any inaccuracies or mistakes, get them fixed as soon as possible.

Good Credit Trumps Good Looks

Good credit is sexy. No, I'm not kidding. If you're looking to impress on a first date, whip out a copy of your credit report (if you don't get a second date, don't blame it; you probably just weren't their type). Sixty-seven percent of Canadian millennials said they'd choose a partner with a good credit score over good looks. If your credit score leaves something to be desired, don't despair. Only 2% said poor credit could lead to a break up. A whopping 87% said they would help their partner improve their credit score.[1] Long live the power of love!

Understanding Your Credit Score

Five main factors affect your credit score. It's important to understand each of them to help maximize it.

1. Payment History

Your payment history has the biggest impact on your credit score. As the saying goes, "The best predictor of future behaviour is past behaviour." Things that can hurt your payment history include missing or making late payments, any debts that have been written off or sent to collections, and filing for bankruptcy. To protect your credit score, pay your bills on time. If you can't pay the full amount, pay at least the minimum payment to keep your credit in good standing.

Maintain a Good Credit Score

Aim for a credit score of 720 or higher for a buffer against accidentally paying your credit card or utility bill late, for instance. Anything below 640 and it's really tough to qualify for a mortgage. You'll need a good explanation for lenders, or else you'll have to deal with alternative lenders, sometimes called *B lenders*. If you've filed for bankruptcy or you have less-than-stellar credit, you may be able to qualify for a mortgage with an alternative lender, albeit with higher mortgage rates and larger down payment requirements.

2. Available Credit

After payment history, *available credit* (also called *credit utilization*) carries the second most weight with lenders. Your total available credit (not your total credit limit) counts toward your credit score. Your available credit is how much credit you have at your disposal. It's your credit limit (how much credit you have available to borrow) minus your current balance.

To determine your total available credit, tally up the credit limits on all your credit products (credit cards, lines of credit and so on). Ideally, you'll want a credit utilization of less than 35%, but never, ever go over 70%, even if you pay off your balance every month. When you're using a higher percentage of your available credit, lenders tend to get nervous and see you as a greater risk, even if you still pay your balance in full and on time. Have more credit than you need and use it responsibly.

For example, if you have a Visa credit card with a limit of $6,000 and a line of credit for $10,000, your total available credit is $16,000. Try not to borrow more than $5,600 at any time (35% of $16,000).

3. Number of Credit Inquiries

When it comes to credit inquiries, there are two types: soft hits and hard hits. *Soft hits*, such as asking for a copy of your credit report, won't impact your credit score. *Hard hits* are inquiries that count toward your credit score.

Whenever you apply for credit, whether it's a credit card or mortgage, lenders ask for a copy of your credit report. When this happens, a credit inquiry is recorded—a hard hit. Inquiries are expected every now and then, but too many over a short period can negatively impact your credit score.

Lenders can see how many credit inquiries have been made. To protect your credit score, limit the number of hard hits. When shopping for a mortgage, apply only at lenders you're serious about. And try to apply for mortgages within a two-week period (these inquiries usually will be lumped together and treated as one).

4. Credit History Length

You may have heard that no credit can be as bad as poor credit. Lenders want to see that you have a track record of making your payments in full and on time. The longer your credit account is open, the more it helps your credit score.

Some people lack a credit history (maybe they've been afraid to sign up for a credit card after the financial crisis, or they're a recent grad or new immigrant). If that's you, take steps to start building your credit history today. Apply for a no-fee credit card and pay it off in full each month. Ideally, have at least two unsecured forms of credit with clean payment histories (paying off your balance in full on time each month) of a minimum of 24 months, with a limit of at least $2,000 each.

5. Types of Credit

Having only a single credit type, like a credit card, can hurt your credit score. Spice up your credit report with different types of credit. Instead of carrying a wallet full of credit cards, replace some of that plastic with a line of credit or personal loan. A word of caution: although it's good to have different credit types, don't go overboard—apply only for credit you truly need.

Pre-qualified vs. Pre-approved: Know the Difference

It's hard to go house hunting if you're not sure how much home you can afford. Mortgage pre-qualifications and pre-approvals help answer that all-important question by telling you how much mortgage you'll qualify for. This can save you time and avoid heartbreak, since you'll know to only look at homes in your price range.

Pre-qualified

Getting pre-qualified is often the first step in applying for a mortgage, and if you're merely toying with the idea of homeownership, it may be the way to go. Your bank will ask for basic personal and financial information, including your income and a list of your assets and debts. It then crunches the numbers and gives you the mortgage amount you qualify for. You don't have to visit a branch to be pre-qualified—you can often do it from the comfort of your home by phone or online.

A mortgage pre-qualification only goes so far (e.g., it doesn't include a credit check). Its main purpose is to give you a ballpark figure of the mortgage you *may* be approved for. Getting pre-qualified but then not pre-approved can be disastrous. The figure is not written in stone. You may think you can buy a home for $500,000, but without a firm commitment, your lender could deny your mortgage pre-approval. If you're serious about buying a home, skip the pre-qualification and get pre-approved.

Pre-approved

Getting pre-approved for a mortgage is the next step (or for some, the first step) in applying for a mortgage. When you're pre-approved, the bank provides a pre-approval commitment in writing.

You'll complete a mortgage application form and provide the bank with identification, such as your driver's licence number, a letter of employment (for salaried employees), tax slips or notices of assessment for the previous two years and financial statements to show the source of your down payment. The bank will want to see a copy of your credit report (this counts as a hard hit—see Number of Credit Inquiries, above). Based on this, the bank will tell you the maximum home price you're approved for. You'll also get a letter stating the mortgage amount, the type and the rate you've been pre-approved for. Of course, you're under no obligation to buy. If you change your mind, you can simply let the pre-approval expire. Pre-approvals typically last between 90 and 120 days (though it varies by lender).

Besides telling you your price range of homes, many banks let you obtain a *rate hold*. A rate hold gives you some peace of mind: if mortgage rates go up while you're searching for a home, with a fixed mortgage, you're guaranteed the rate you were pre-approved for. If rates go down, you get the lower rate. It's a win-win situation for homebuyers. For a variable-rate mortgage, you're guaranteed the spread (the difference between your mortgage rate and the lender's prime rate*).

Keep an Eye on Mortgage Rates
Consider choosing a different mortgage type if mortgage rates change a lot since you were pre-approved. For example, if variable-rate mortgages are a lot lower when the home purchase closes, you might decide to go with variable instead of fixed.

A pre-approval is a great learning opportunity. Your banker will talk to you about the mortgage types that best suit your needs. When you're pre-approved for a mortgage and find your dream home, you can make an offer with confidence.

Being pre-approved means you're financially ready to buy a home; it doesn't guarantee you a mortgage. The missing piece of the puzzle is the property. Is it in fair to good condition, with an economic life of at least 30 years? Did you pay fair value? Does the home have asbestos or other environmental or safety issues? Your lender wants to know it's investing in a rock-solid asset before approving your mortgage.

Has Your Pre-approval Hit a Snag?

If you're having trouble getting pre-approved or you're unhappy about how much mortgage you qualify for, don't despair. Here are some things you can do to improve your chances of being approved:

---

* *Prime rate* is the interest rate offered by lenders on loans to their most creditworthy (or "prime") borrowers.

- **Boost your income and down payment.** Look for a job with a higher starting salary, ask for a raise or get a part-time job.

- **Set realistic home-buying expectations.** Instead of buying a house, look at more affordable options, like a condo or townhouse.

- **Pay down your debt.** Make a plan to aggressively pay down any consumer debt you have, whether it's credit cards or a line of credit.

- **Improve your credit score.** This is related to paying down your debts. Make your debt payments in full and on time.

- **Get a co-signer.** If you lack credit or you're self-employed, getting someone to co-sign and guarantee your mortgage can be helpful.

Qualifying for a Mortgage When You're Self-Employed

Qualifying for a mortgage can be challenging when you're self-employed. Self-employed people make up about 15% of the Canadian workforce (this number is expected to grow in the coming years). When you're self-employed, you have the added hurdle of proving you have the ability to repay your mortgage.

Lenders are looking for steady income—a small business owner with stable earnings over several years will likely have an easier time qualifying for a mortgage than will a freelancer whose income fluctuates monthly. Having a steady rental history, decent credit score and low debt ratios can go a long way toward getting pre-approved.

If you're seeking a mortgage with your partner, it helps if they are a salaried employee. If you're using stated income, you'll need to provide further documentation, such as financial statements, client contracts and recent notices of assessment. You'll also need a heftier down payment, and higher mortgage insurance premiums will apply. You may have to pay a mortgage insurance premium right up to a 35% down payment. This can be quite costly. For that reason, the greater your down payment, the better.

Getting It in Writing: Your Mortgage Commitment

The mortgage commitment is the third and final stage in the mortgage-approval process. It happens when the offer you made on a home is accepted. Your bank will want to verify your finances one last time to make sure nothing has changed (e.g., that you still have steady income and haven't lost your down payment in the stock market). If your credit history was pulled more than 30 days ago, it'll also pull a new report. To make sure you're paying a reasonable price for the home, you may be required to get an appraisal done (at your expense; more on this later). If everything checks out, your mortgage will be approved.

Are Mortgages Sexist?

When men and women head to the bank to get a mortgage, who's more likely to get the better deal? Studies in the U.S. and U.K. have found that women generally pay higher mortgage rates than men with similar income.[2] I suspect the findings in Canada are similar. Why? Although gender discrimination is a factor, it seems that women don't shop around enough for their mortgage. In fact, women are more likely to act on a friend's recommendation, whereas men are more likely to speak with a mortgage broker. Since a mortgage is quite possibly the largest debt of your lifetime, I strongly encourage you, no matter your gender, to shop around with a broker. (Don't worry, you won't hurt your banker's feelings—you might even get a lower mortgage rate with the bank this way.)

How Mortgage Payments Work

Paying off your mortgage sooner is a lot easier if you understand how mortgage payments work. Mortgage payments consist of two main parts: principal and interest. When you make a mortgage payment, some of the money goes toward principal, some of it toward interest. *Principal* is the amount of money borrowed from the bank for your mortgage. *Interest* is the money your bank earns on the money you've borrowed.

To get a better understanding of your mortgage, it helps to take a look at your *amortization schedule*, the table that summarizes your mortgage payments. Mortgage interest is front-loaded. New homeowners are often shocked to learn that at the start of their mortgage, even at today's low mortgage rates, almost half of payments will go toward interest, not principal. As you pay down the mortgage, more of your money goes toward principal and less toward interest.

EXAMPLE AMORTIZATION SCHEDULE

To illustrate how mortgage payments work, let's look at a mortgage amortization schedule. The lender will likely provide you with one when you sign up for a mortgage. It gives you a breakdown of mortgage payments (including the split of interest and principal) over your amortization period, which is the length of time it takes to fully repay your mortgage.

For our example, let's use a $300,000 mortgage at 2.99% paid accelerated biweekly over 25 years. In the first payment, you'll notice that almost half of the mortgage goes to interest, with the other half going to principal (even more money would go toward interest if the mortgage rate was higher, which is just another reason to pay down the mortgage sooner before rates go up). With each mortgage payment, more money goes toward principal and less toward interest. At around year 15, over four times the money goes toward principal versus interest. In the last full mortgage payment, a measly $1.04 goes toward interest.

Payment date	Payment amount ($)	Interest ($)	Principal ($)	Balance ($)
Feb 1, 2017 (1st payment)	709.10	342.64	366.46	299,633.54
Feb 9, 2022 (approx. 5 years)	709.10	283.53	425.57	247,822.79
Feb 3, 2027 (approx. 10 years)	709.10	215.46	493.64	188,149.58
Feb 11, 2032 (approx. 15 years)	709.10	135.84	573.26	118,357.20
Feb 4, 2037 (approx. 20 years)	709.10	44.13	664.97	37,973.55
Mar 16, 2039 (last full payment)	709.10	1.04	708.06	206.19

Nobody wants most of their hard-earned money going toward interest instead of principal. So how do you cut down on the amount of interest you pay? By taking advantage of mortgage prepayments (more on this below). Low mortgage rates let us qualify for bigger mortgages; they also let us pay down our mortgage faster. Here's why: the lower your mortgage rate, the more your money goes toward principal and the less toward interest. The sunny days of low mortgage rates won't last forever. Instead of using low mortgage rates to buy more home, take advantage of them to pay down your mortgage faster.

Why Use a Non-bank Lender?

When I first started looking for a mortgage, I did what any first-time home-buyer would do: I went straight to my local bank branch. After shopping the market with a broker, I discovered my bank wasn't giving me the best rate. I ended up getting a mortgage with a non-bank lender. Not only did this lender give me a lower mortgage rate, it has a less costly mortgage penalty and more generous prepayment privileges.

Many people are shy about shopping for a mortgage outside the big banks. Non-traditional lenders with a solid track record are worth considering, especially if it means paying down your mortgage sooner. Even if you sign up with your bank, at least you'll have the peace of mind knowing you're getting a decent mortgage rate.

Shopping for a Mortgage: Brokers vs. Banks

Buying a home is a busy time. Between house hunting, daily errands, picking the kids up from school and dealing with your agent and lawyer, you'll need to find time to go mortgage hunting. Some people will spend more time shopping for the perfect phone than their mortgage. Your mortgage is most likely the largest debt of your lifetime. Taking the time to shop for it is time well spent. With mortgage-rate comparison websites like RateHub.ca, RateSpy.com, RateSupermarket.ca and LowestRates.ca, it's easier than ever to compare mortgages. A mortgage rate even 0.1% or 0.2% lower can mean saving thousands of dollars in interest over the life of the mortgage.

There are two main places to shop for a mortgage: at your bank or with a mortgage broker. Brokers are popular in Canada—about half of new mortgages were obtained through a broker in 2015.[3] Consider these points when deciding between brokers and banks.

Mortgage Brokers

Pros

• **Time and money saver:** Using a broker is a lot like using the express checkout at the supermarket. Brokers save you time and money by looking at the mortgages that best suit your financial situation.

• **Lower rate:** Through a broker, you can often get a rate lower than you would get if you went directly to a bank. Some lenders offer lower rates exclusively to brokers.

• **Unbiased advice:** Brokers are able to offer unbiased opinions. They are typically paid the same by each lender, so they have no vested interest when it comes to recommending the best product.

• **No cost:** Typically, you won't be charged fees for a broker's services—the lender usually pays the broker when your home purchase closes. (However, you may be charged fees if you have poor credit history or no credit experience in Canada.)

• **Protect your credit score:** Mortgage brokers know how to shop around among lenders without each inquiry counting as a hard hit. Since your broker only has to request your credit report once, your credit score is protected.

• **Greater choice:** Brokers deal with a wide variety of lenders, including banks, credit unions, trust companies, private lenders and pension funds. They have a better chance of finding the best mortgage for you.

• **Flexible hours:** Many brokers offer more flexible hours than banks (I spoke with my broker on weekends while he was at his cottage). Often, you can deal with your broker over the phone and the Internet without ever meeting face to face.

Cons

• **Look out for yourself:** Although most brokers are honest, there's always the risk that your broker could encourage you to sign up for a mortgage with a higher rate to pocket a heftier commission. So pay extra attention to the mortgage's annual percentage rate on the mortgage approval (brokers are forced to show you this). If the mortgage rate is 2.99% but a fee is tacked on to bring it up to 3.99%, that's a red flag! Before signing on the dotted line, ask your broker, "Is this the lowest mortgage rate available?" And don't just take their word for it—spend 10 minutes checking a mortgage-rate comparison website to make sure you can't find a lower rate.

- **Broker discrimination:** Some lenders won't deal directly with brokers, so you may still need to shop the market on your own.

Banks

Pros

- **Perks:** Your bank may throw in perks like a no-fee chequing account or may waive the home appraisal fee.

- **Extra services:** Banks often offer extra services like mortgage planning and home-buying seminars.

- **Stability:** You can rest easy knowing that if you get a mortgage with the big banks, they aren't likely to go belly up.

- **Personal service:** It can be convenient to stroll to your local bank branch. You can meet your banker face to face to discuss your mortgage needs.

Cons

- **Less choice:** The bank can only recommend mortgages it offers. You'll need to look out for your own best interests. The bank isn't likely to tell you there's a better-suited mortgage at their competitor.

- **Time needed:** We're all busy. It takes a lot of time to visit several banks and apply in person.

- **Lower credit score:** Applying at too many banks can lower your credit score (because of the number of hard hits). It's best to apply only to those you're serious about using.

- **Negotiating:** You'll have to haggle with your bank for the lowest rate. Your bank may not be willing to budge on the posted rate unless you prove to them you can get a better rate elsewhere.

- **Less expertise:** Bankers may not be as knowledgeable as brokers about mortgages because they deal with a variety of financial products, rather than focusing on mortgages.

- **Higher mortgage penalties:** This is especially relevant if you're signing up for a fixed-rate mortgage. The big banks calculate fixed-rate penalties using their posted rates. This can lead to a hefty mortgage penalty if you break your mortgage (more on this below).

There's More to a Mortgage Than Just the Rate

Shopping for a mortgage is a lot more than simply finding the mortgage with the lowest rate. You wouldn't shop for a condo by lowest list price only, ignoring other factors like maintenance fees, amenities and location. So don't do it with your mortgage. The lowest mortgage rate *may* be the best mortgage, but there's no guarantee. Although a slightly lower mortgage rate can help you save thousands of dollars in interest over the life of the mortgage, it may not be worth it. It may come with restrictions like stiffer mortgage penalties, limited prepayment privileges and shorter closing times (some lenders offer a lower rate when your mortgage closes in 30 to 45 days). In some cases, it can actually make sense to choose a mortgage with a slightly higher rate (e.g., 0.10% to 0.20% higher than the lowest available rate). So do your homework: you might be better off with a mortgage with a slightly higher rate and better prepayment privileges, say.

Here are four important factors besides the rate.

1. Penalties: Breaking a Mortgage Doesn't Come Cheap

When you sign up for a mortgage, breaking it is probably the last thing on your mind. But sometimes life happens—you get sick, lose your job or accept a promotion in another city—and you end up breaking it. In Canada, where the five-year fixed-rate mortgage reigns supreme, about 70% of people change their mortgage before the end of its term.[4] Given that the odds are stacked against you, take the time to ask your lender about any penalties before signing up for the mortgage. Mortgage penalties are meant to compensate your bank for lost interest.

In Canada, mortgage penalties depend on the type of mortgage. If you have a variable-rate mortgage, you'll pay three months' interest, but if you have a fixed-rate mortgage, you'll pay the greater of three months' interest or something called the *interest rate differential* (IRD for short). The IRD is calculated by looking at current mortgage rates and your remaining mortgage balance.

If you're signing up for a fixed-rate mortgage, ask how the IRD is calculated. Is it based on the posted or the discount rate? If it's based on the lender's inflated posted rate, consider this carefully before signing up. Your mortgage penalty could add up to thousands of dollars. If you do decide to break your mortgage, prepay as much of it as you can to reduce your penalty.

Avoiding Costly Mortgage Penalties
If you're unsure whether you plan to stay at the property long term, take a shorter-term or variable-rate mortgage to avoid hefty mortgage penalties, or rent instead.

EXAMPLE FIXED-RATE MORTGAGE PENALTIES: THREE MONTHS' INTEREST VS. THE IRD

To understand the difference in mortgage penalties, let's run through a couple of examples. Samantha purchases a condo for $375,000 in Calgary. She signs up for a five-year fixed-rate mortgage, like most Canadians do. A couple of years later, Samantha accepts a fantastic job offer in Toronto. She decides to sell her condo in Calgary and rent in Toronto, since she wants to make sure she likes it there before buying. Samantha has a 2.99% five-year fixed-rate mortgage, with an outstanding mortgage balance of $300,000. Using *three months' interest*, Samantha's mortgage penalty would be:

$$2.99\% \times \$300{,}000 \times (3\text{ months}/12\text{ months}) = \$2{,}243$$

However, Samantha signed up for a five-year fixed-rate mortgage, so she also must calculate her penalty using the IRD. Although Samantha's mortgage rate is only 2.99%, her lender uses the rate of 4.79%, the posted rate when she signed up for her mortgage, to calculate the mortgage penalty. Samantha has three years (36 months) left on her mortgage. Her lender's current three-year fixed mortgage rate is 2.59%. Using the IRD, Samantha's mortgage penalty would be:

$$\$300{,}000 \times 36\text{ months} \times 2.20\% \text{ (the difference}$$
$$\text{between } 4.79\% \text{ and } 2.59\%)/12\text{ months} = \$19{,}800$$

Since the IRD in this example is greater than three months' interest, to break her mortgage, Samantha would have to pay nearly $20,000 (the price of a new car!). This is why it's crucial to ask about mortgage penalties *before* signing up for your mortgage.

2. Prepayment Privileges

If you'd like to pay down your mortgage sooner rather than later, prepayment privileges are a must. Banks are pretty flexible with payment privileges. Most let you prepay, each year, between 10% and 20% of your original mortgage balance as a lump sum. This is only one prepayment option. Others include increasing your payment and doubling up your payment.

When shopping for a mortgage, ask which prepayment privileges are offered and the percentage you can prepay. With my lender, after my mortgage anniversary (the date I signed up for the mortgage), each year I could increase my payment by 15%, double up my payments and make lump-sum payments totalling 15% of my original mortgage balance. Unlike regular mortgage payments, which are split between interest and principal, prepayments go straight toward principal. Prepayments can shave years off your mortgage and save thousands of dollars in interest over the life of your mortgage.

3. Portability

Portability means your mortgage can come with you if you decide to move—that is, you can transfer the mortgage to your new property. If you're buying a more expensive home, you may be able to "blend and extend" the mortgage by combining your existing mortgage with the mortgage for your new home. Portability is a great feature—it can save you from paying thousands of dollars in mortgage penalties. It also helps if your mortgage is *assumable*. With an assumable mortgage, you can leave it behind for a new qualified buyer instead of breaking it, avoiding costly mortgage penalties.

4. Standard vs. Collateral Charge

Before signing up, find out if the mortgage has a standard or collateral charge. Mortgage loans are secured against real property, and it's the *charge*, registered with the province against your property, that gives the lender the right to sell your property if you don't repay the loan according to the terms. A *standard charge* secures only the mortgage loan—not any other loans you have with that lender, like a line of credit. What this means in part is that you can leave your mortgage at the end of its term and not pay any significant fees (e.g., the discharge fee of approximately $300). A *collateral charge*, on the other hand, enables you to secure other loans with your lender. It makes it easier for a HELOC down the road (more on HELOCs in chapter 11), but you will need to pay legal and appraisal fees to get out of it (legal and appraisal fees of approximately $1,400, if not more, and a discharge fee of approximately $300). When you have a collateral charge, the bank doesn't have to offer you its best rate upon renewal (more on mortgage renewals in chapter 11).

Fixed vs. Variable Rate

Soup or salad? Cream or sugar? Fixed or variable? The decision to go with a fixed-rate mortgage versus a variable-rate mortgage is important. Since a mortgage is the single largest debt for most families, the type of mortgage you choose can have a major bearing on how soon you reach mortgage freedom.

Fixed Rate

If you're a first-time homebuyer or risk-averse (the stock market keeps you up at night), a *fixed-rate mortgage* may be the way to go. With a fixed-rate mortgage, your mortgage rate and payment stay the same during the mortgage term. Signing up for a fixed-rate mortgage is often referred to as "locking in." A fixed-rate mortgage makes budgeting easier, since you don't have to worry about your mortgage payments going up until renewal. However, this comes at a cost—fixed-rate mortgages typically come with higher mortgage rates than do variable-rate mortgages. In Canada, five-year fixed-rate mortgages are most popular.

Variable Rate

For those looking to pay down their mortgage sooner, a *variable-rate mortgage* may be your best bet. You'll typically get a lower mortgage rate on variable than on fixed. However, there are downsides—your mortgage rate and payment can change during your mortgage term when the bank hikes or lowers its prime rate (this often happens when the Bank of Canada changes the overnight lending rate*). Although you usually have the opportunity to lock in at the fixed rate (you may want to do this when rates start to rise), by that time they may have already gone up quite a lot. Your bank is also not likely to offer you its best fixed rate, since your only other choice is to break your mortgage and pay a penalty.

Variable-rate mortgages make the most sense when interest rates stay the same or fall. A study found that homeowners would come out ahead 9 times out of 10 by going variable instead of fixed.[5] (Keep in mind that this study took place during a period when interest rates were primarily falling.) If you believe interest rates are going up, you may be better off with a fixed-rate mortgage. If you're planning to pay down your mortgage in five years or less, a variable-rate mortgage may make the most sense, but if it will take you longer, a fixed-rate mortgage is worth considering.

• • • • •

5 Key Mortgage-Burning Takeaways

➤ **Learn the rules of the game.** Lenders use four main mortgage qualification factors: income, down payment, debt ratios and credit score. Know them and use them to your advantage.

➤ **Review your credit report**. Request a free copy of your credit report and your credit score *before* applying for a mortgage. If you find any inaccuracies or mistakes in your credit report, take the necessary steps to get them fixed pronto.

---

* The *overnight lending rate* is the interest rate at which major financial institutions borrow and lend one-day funds among themselves. It's often referred to as the *benchmark* or *key interest rate*.

➤ **Get pre-approved.** A mortgage pre-approval saves you time and avoids heartbreak because you'll know the price range of homes you can afford. Many pre-approvals come with the added bonus of a rate hold, which helps protect you if mortgage rates go up while you're house hunting.

➤ **Shop around for a mortgage.** Your local bank branch may be your first stop, but it shouldn't be your only stop. Weigh the pros and cons of going with a bank versus a broker to get the mortgage that's best suited for you.

➤ **Consider all the factors when mortgage shopping.** The lowest mortgage rate isn't necessarily the best mortgage. Consider other factors like prepayments, penalties and portability.

> *Once you get the kids raised and the mortgage paid*
> *off and accomplish what you wanted to do in life,*
> *there's a great feeling of: "Hey, I'm free as a bird."*
> DICK VAN DYKE, actor

11

Making the Most of Your Mortgage Payments
Achieving Financial Freedom Sooner

HAVE YOU EVER wondered what the origin of the word *mortgage* is? The English word comes from the French *mort-gage*, which translates as "death-pledge." French peasants literally worked themselves to death to own a home. (Boy, they weren't kidding about a mortgage being a life sentence!)

Your mortgage may seem like a death pledge, but it doesn't have to be. In the previous chapter you learned everything you needed to know to find the best mortgage for you. In this chapter you'll learn what you need to know to pay it off, so that you can have a mortgage-burning party of your own.

Seven Simple Ways to Pay Down Your Mortgage Sooner

This is the moment you've all been waiting for. Below you'll find simple ways to burn your mortgage. To make things easier, we'll use the same fictional mortgage in each example discussed below. So, imagine you're buying a condo for $375,000 with a 20% down payment ($75,000), leaving you with a $300,000 mortgage. Like most Canadians, you go with the safety of a five-year fixed-rate mortgage at 2.99%. Instead of monthly, you choose to pay your mortgage accelerated biweekly.

1. Accelerating Your Mortgage Payments

There's a common misconception about payment frequency. Many people think that how often they make a mortgage payment plays a larger role in interest savings than it actually does (in fact, it plays a small role.) It's the *accelerated* alternatives that save you the big bucks. When you pay weekly (52 payments per year) or biweekly (26 payments per year) instead of monthly (12 payments per year), the interest savings are minimal; in these scenarios, it's more about finding the payment frequency that best matches your cash flow. With *accelerated* weekly (52 payments per year) and biweekly (26 payments per year), you're paying the equivalent of an extra month's payment every year (more on this below).

At first glance, you're probably wondering how you're saving any interest with accelerated weekly or biweekly. After all, you're still making the same number of payments as non-accelerated weekly and biweekly. While that may be true, you're actually paying a slightly higher amount on each mortgage payment. To understand this, it helps to look at the difference in the way biweekly and accelerated biweekly are calculated.

If your monthly mortgage payment is $1,418 and you pay biweekly, your biweekly payment is $654 ($1,418 × 12 months/26 weeks = $654). But when you pay accelerated biweekly, your biweekly payment is slightly higher, at $709 ($1,418 × 12 months/24 weeks = $709). As mentioned, with accelerated weekly and biweekly, you're paying the equivalent of 13 monthly mortgage payments instead of only 12.

Paying accelerated on a biweekly schedule that matches your payday is the most painless way to budget for the higher payment. You won't even realize you're making higher annual payments (it's probably a good thing, as you might not choose this option if you did).

EXAMPLE ACCELERATE YOUR MORTGAGE PAYMENTS AND SAVE BIG BUCKS

Accelerating your mortgage payments can make a big difference compared with regular (i.e., non-accelerated) payment frequency. As the chart below shows, by paying your mortgage accelerated biweekly instead of monthly, you can save over $15,000 in interest and pay off your mortgage almost three years sooner.

Payment frequency	Payment amount ($)	Total interest paid ($)	Interest saved ($)	Years to mortgage freedom
Monthly	1,418	125,459	0	25
Biweekly	654	125,175	284	25
Weekly	327	125,051	407	25
Accelerated biweekly	709	110,066	15,393	22.27
Accelerated weekly	355	109,901	15,558	22.25

2. Make Lump-Sum Payments

Make lump-sum payments whenever you can afford to (most lenders let you do this on one of your regular payment dates during each year of the mortgage term) by tossing "found" money—tax refunds, bonuses, cash gifts—at your mortgage. Look for new ways to save money: brownbag your lunch, switch to a less expensive cell-phone plan or carpool, and put the money you save toward a lump-sum payment on your mortgage. Lump-sum payments go straight toward principal, saving thousands of dollars in interest and shaving years off your mortgage amortization. For example, if you take your $2,000 bonus at work and make a lump-sum payment each year with it, you'll save $17,774 in interest and pay off your mortgage in only 19 years—6 years sooner.

3. Shorten the Amortization Period

By shortening your amortization period—the length of time it takes to fully repay the mortgage—your mortgage payment will be higher, but you can save a ton in interest. Try shortening your amortization period from 25 years to 20 years. In the same example, by paying your mortgage in 20 years instead of 25 years, not only will you pay off you mortgage 5 years sooner, you'll save $22,891 in interest.

That being said, to give yourself more flexibility, you might consider going with a longer amortization period and taking full advantage of your prepayment privileges. That way, if you lose your job, say, you won't be stuck paying the higher mortgage payment. At the time of writing, the maximum amortization for a high-ratio mortgage is 25 years, and 30 years for a conventional mortgage.

4. Round Up Your Mortgage Payments

Round up your mortgage payments to the closest $25 payment increment, so you're paying a few extra dollars a month toward your mortgage. By rounding $709 paid accelerated biweekly up to $725—$16 more (about the price of a couple of beers at happy hour)—you'll save $3,697 in interest and pay off your mortgage in just less than 22 years—3 years sooner. Get in the good habit of increasing your mortgage payment whenever you get a raise at work or land a lucrative long-term contract.

Don't Get Dinged with NSF Charges

Keep track of money coming out of your chequing account for mortgage prepayments. Consider making purchases on your credit card instead of your debit card so you don't have to worry about your bank account balance before each purchase (that being said, be careful not to carry a balance on your credit card, as the interest is costly).

5. Pay Your Mortgage as If Rates Are Higher

By increasing your mortgage payment as if rates are 2% or 3% higher than they are, not only will you pay your mortgage off sooner, you'll be prepared if mortgages rates are higher when your mortgage comes up for renewal. If you pay your mortgage as if rates are 4.99% (i.e., 2% higher), your biweekly accelerated payments will increase from $709 to $872. Although your payments would be $163 more, you'd save $28,719 in interest and pay off your mortgage in less than 17 years.

6. Consider Refinancing Your Mortgage

If mortgage rates are a lot lower today than they were when you signed up for your mortgage, it may be worth refinancing it. When you refinance your mortgage, you're breaking your existing mortgage to sign up for a new mortgage at a lower rate. This often comes with penalties and fees (see Standard vs. Collateral Charge, p. 136). To come out ahead, your savings from refinancing have to outweigh the penalties (see the example in chapter 10, Penalties: Breaking a Mortgage Doesn't Come Cheap). Before you break your mortgage, get your mortgage broker to crunch the numbers, or use an online mortgage-penalty calculator to make sure it makes sense to do so (your mortgage penalty could end up being higher than you think). To reduce the mortgage penalty, prepay as much of the mortgage as you can before breaking it. To save even more interest, when you refinance, keep paying the same mortgage payment you were paying at the previous higher rate. As for fees, ask your new lender to see if they'll cover them.

Contributing to an RRSP vs. Paying Down Your Mortgage

There's a never-ending debate about whether it's better to pay down your mortgage or contribute to an RRSP. Keep things simple. Contributing to an RRSP doesn't make sense for everyone (e.g., if you expect your tax rate to be higher in retirement than it is now), but for those for whom it does, contribute to it and use the tax refund as a lump-sum payment on your mortgage.

7. Set a Mortgage-Free Date and Celebrate Your Accomplishment

I wouldn't have paid off my mortgage in three years by age 30 if I hadn't set a mortgage-free date. It all comes down to goal setting. I'm a sci-fi nerd, so I wanted to pay off my mortgage before *Star Wars: The Force Awakens* hit theatres. I'm not ashamed to admit I had a *Star Wars* countdown clock on Facebook—every morning I'd wake up to see how many days were left until the movie's release. This helped motivate me to keep going.

Circle the date of your mortgage-burning party on the calendar (and complete the worksheet below), and do what it takes to pay off your mortgage early (heck, send out invitations early if that's going to motivate you!). Imagine how amazing it will be to celebrate burning your mortgage with all your family and friends cheering you on.

Your Mortgage-Free Action Plan

Setting the goal of being mortgage-free is a good first step. You'll need to take the steps to achieve it. Here's an action plan template to help you get started. Choose a mortgage-free date and work your way backwards to figure out by how much you need to boost your income and cut your expenses.

My mortgage-free date is: _____

To reach my mortgage-free date:
I'm going to boost my **income** by $ _____ per month by (mark with a check):
☐ Asking for a raise at work
☐ Getting a part-time job
☐ Doing side hustle (see the appendix for creative ideas)
☐ Renting out my home to tenants (see chapter 14)

I'm going to cut my **spending** by $____ per month (fill in the amount from the How Much Money Could You Be Saving? worksheet in chapter 2).

With the money I'm saving, to pay off my mortgage early, I'm going to:
Increase my payment frequency to (mark with a check):
☐ Accelerated biweekly
☐ Accelerated weekly
Make **lump-sum payments** of $ _____ per year
Shorten my **amortization period** to _____ years
Increase my mortgage payments to $ _____

Once I reach financial freedom, I plan to (mark with a check):
☐ Spend more time with family and friends
☐ Travel the world
☐ Volunteer
☐ Take up a new hobby
☐ Write a book
☐ Get in better shape
☐ All of the above

How I Paid Off My Mortgage in Just Three Years

When I bought my house, I signed up for a five-year fixed-rate mortgage at 3.04% with the help of a mortgage broker. I went with a longer amortization period (30 years) to give myself more of a safety net in case I had a financial emergency. I took advantage of all the prepayment privileges my lender offered—I paid my mortgage accelerated weekly, doubled up payments, made lump-sum payments with freelance and rental income and increased my payments yearly. I maximized my prepayment privileges every single year, until I had paid off my mortgage just over three years later.

HELOCs: Avoid Turning Your Home into an ATM

A HELOC, short for "home equity line of credit," is a revolving line of credit secured by your home's equity. HELOCs have a reputation for being a convenient, flexible and low-cost way of accessing credit. A HELOC can be a great way to borrow money cheaply (it sure beats using your credit card!), but if you're not careful, you can find yourself with a bigger mortgage than when you started.

With home prices heading into the stratosphere and low interest rates since the 2008 financial crisis, homeowners are taking out HELOCs in droves. Dubbed the "HGTV effect," homeowners are spending millions on renos after watching shows on the speciality channel.[1] Canadian homeowners spent a record $63.4 billion in home renovations in 2013.[2]

It may make sense to use a HELOC for renovations that will increase your home's resale value, but very few renovations fit that bill. If you're finishing your basement to rent out to a tenant, this can be a good use of a HELOC, but besides that, you'll be hard-pressed to find renos that provide a positive return on investment (despite what the home renovation shows on HGTV say).[3]

The real danger in HELOCs is our own behaviour. You can turn your home into an ATM, withdrawing money whenever you feel like it. The flexible repayment terms make it easy to fall into this trap. Most

HELOCs let you make interest-only payments. This can maximize your cash flow, but it's not a good idea if you want to be mortgage-free (and you're reading this book, aren't you?). You can get into a vicious cycle of making interest-only payments and not chipping away at the principal.

Although a HELOC can be a great way to consolidate debt and pay it down at a lower interest rate, use it and abuse it and it may cost you dearly. Using your HELOC to finance a lifestyle you can't afford will catch up with you eventually. I've seen people use their HELOCs for everything from a family vacation to installing an in-ground swimming pool.

Getting the Biggest Bang for Your Home-Reno Buck
If you're thinking about renovating your home, the kitchen and bathroom tend to provide the best home-reno return on investment. Although a swimming pool can be a lot of fun, it doesn't usually provide much value (and can actually hurt the resale value of your home).

HELOCs typically come with variable interest rates at a much lower rate than unsecured lines of credit. Your interest rate is based on your bank's prime rate. When interest rates rise, so will your monthly payment. Unless you have a crystal ball, there's no way to predict when interest rates will go up. You could find that your new monthly payment is squeezing your cash flow. Falling behind on your HELOC payment can lead to a lower credit score and add to the interest you'll owe. (Be sure to ask if there's a maximum interest rate; if interest rates shoot up, your HELOC could end up costing you an arm and a leg.)

Before tapping into your HELOC, consider what you'll be using the funds for. If it's for something that will boost your net worth, then by all means go ahead, but if you're using it for an ocean kitchen aquarium, you may want to think twice. If you decide to borrow money using your HELOC, only borrow as much as you need. Set up a payment plan immediately—try to repay at least a few hundred dollars per month. Since the interest rate on your HELOC will likely be higher than that on your mortgage, toss any extra money you have against your HELOC. You can also typically lock in your HELOC, much like a variable-rate mortgage. This is something to check on if you plan to borrow a significant amount and not pay it down aggressively (though I wouldn't encourage this if your plan is to be mortgage-free).

EXAMPLE HOW MUCH CAN YOU BORROW FROM YOUR HELOC?

With a HELOC, you can access up to 65% of your home's appraised value. Note that your mortgage balance and HELOC together can't be more than 80% of your home's appraised value.

For example, let's say your home's appraised value is $500,000 and you have a $200,000 mortgage.

Home's appraised value = $500,000
Maximum for HELOC and mortgage balance (80% of appraised value)
= $400,000

−

Mortgage balance: $200,000

HELOC credit limit = $200,000

In this example, you'd qualify for a HELOC of $200,000. As you pay off your mortgage and your home's appraised value goes up, you'll be able to borrow more. If you were mortgage-free, you'd be able to borrow up to $325,000 (65% of your home's appraised value; $500,000 × 65%).

Why a Mortgage Vacation Could Be Your Most Expensive Vacation Ever

What's better than a relaxing vacation to somewhere warm during the winter? Picture yourself driving along the beautiful California coastline. I don't mean to burst your bubble—while you may have the vacation part right, you're forgetting the mortgage part. Some lenders offer a *mortgage vacation* (sometimes called a "skip a payment"), which lets you miss your mortgage payment if you have a financial emergency.

While skipping your mortgage payment is better than losing your home and damaging your credit score, going on a mortgage vacation can prove costly. That's because your lender keeps charging you interest. Not only can this end up costing you thousands of dollars in interest (ouch!), it can extend the amortization period of your mortgage (double ouch!).

Instead of going on a mortgage vacation, you're better off planning ahead. Save a rainy-day fund of three to six months' living expenses in a high-interest savings account. That way, if you lose your job or get sick, you'll have the money waiting for you.

Mortgage Up for Renewal? Do Your Homework

If you want to burn your mortgage, you have to be willing to shop the market, especially when your mortgage comes up for renewal. When you get your mortgage renewal offer, do you:

A: Accept the renewal rate offered by your bank?
or
B: See what else is out there to find a better deal?

You may be surprised to hear that many people choose option A. Over one-quarter (27%) of Canadian mortgage holders automatically renew their mortgages when the term is up.[4]

Banks spend millions on advertising and marketing to attract new customers, so the last thing they want is to lose current customers. Banks make it as easy as possible for you to renew your mortgage, but what your bank isn't telling you is that you're probably not getting the best rate. A 2011 Bank of Canada study backs this up. It found that first-time homebuyers and people who switch banks are more likely to get a better deal on their mortgages than those renewing.[5]

We're told never to accept the posted rate, yet so many of us are doing just that when our mortgages come up for renewal. When you receive your lender's renewal offer, whatever you do, don't sign it! Lenders almost never put their best rate on the renewal. Sometimes you'll get a lower mortgage rate simply by phoning your lender and asking for one. A lower mortgage rate could mean saving thousands of dollars in interest over the life of your mortgage.

Your mortgage renewal is too important to leave until the last minute. Start shopping early—four to six months ahead of when your mortgage term ends. This gives you plenty of time to see what else is out there. Get a helping hand: have your mortgage broker's number on speed dial. Your current mortgage may have been the best one for you back when you signed up, but better deals may be out there by the time your mortgage comes up for renewal. Let a broker shop the market on your behalf. Mortgage-rate comparison websites like RateHub.ca, RateSpy.com, RateSupermarket.ca and LowestRates.ca also make shopping for a mortgage a breeze.

• • • • •

5 Key Mortgage-Burning Takeaways

➤ **Accelerate your mortgage payments.** Switching from monthly to accelerated biweekly is the most painless way to save a ton in interest and pay off your mortgage years sooner.

➤ **Make lump-sum payments.** Toss "found" money, such as tax refunds, bonuses and cash gifts, at your mortgage. Lump-sum payments go straight toward principal, saving you thousands of dollars in interest over the life of your mortgage.

➤ **Set a mortgage-free date.** Set your mortgage-free date and come up with an action plan to achieve it. Figure out ways to boost your income and cut your expenses.

➤ **Don't treat your HELOC like an ATM.** Borrowing to pay for renovating your basement apartment to rent to tenants is usually a good investment. Using your HELOC for a vacation or big-screen TV—not so much.

➤ **Shop the market before your mortgage comes up for renewal.** Do this four to six months before the renewal date. Don't accept your bank's initial renewal offer without seeing what else is out there.

*Find the home inspector, and the best home
inspector you can find before you look for a house.*
MIKE HOLMES, celebrity handyman

12

Closing Costs
and Disbursements
The Hidden Costs
of Real Estate

THE BIGGEST SURPRISE for me as a first-time homebuyer was the closing costs. After I spent $500 on a home inspection, I thought the worst was over. Wrong. Real estate lawyer fees, municipal and provincial land transfer taxes, title insurance, appraisal fee—the list went on and the expenses added up. Before I knew it, I had spent a few thousand dollars in closing costs. Luckily for me, my mortgage broker recommended that I hold back some money from the down payment for what he called the "hidden costs of real estate." I was almost blindsided by closing costs, but fortunately I had the cash on hand to cover them. I've spoken with many first-time homebuyers and it seems that my experience is not unique.

In this chapter I'll break down the most common closing costs you'll face as a buyer, so you aren't caught off guard. You'll also learn how to hire an expert home inspector and the MVP on your team, your lawyer. Plus I'll also help you determine whether to DIY or hire help for the big move.

Closing Costs and Disbursements—How Much?

Closing costs and disbursements, the fees paid when a real estate deal closes, are often referred to as the hidden cost of real estate. *Closing costs* are legal and administrative costs you'll need to cover when your home closes—lawyer fees, municipal and provincial land transfer taxes, title insurance, appraisal fee—whereas *disbursements* are paid to your lawyer to cover out-of-pocket expenses such as registrations, searches and photocopies. I know what you're thinking: How much? Closing costs typically add up to between 1.5% and 4% of a home's purchase price. If you're making only the minimum 5% down payment, closing costs can almost be as much as your down payment.

To see how much closing costs can add up to, let's run through an example. If you're buying a $500,000 home, budget up to $20,000 (4%) toward closing costs. That's almost as much as a new car!

The good news for first-time homebuyers is that you may catch a break on some of your closing costs. Buying a home is expensive. To encourage more people to become homeowners, many provincial governments offer first-time homebuyers rebates on land transfer taxes. These rebates can mean thousands of dollars in tax savings, so take advantage of them (more on this below).

Top Three Closing-Cost Tips

1 Remember to budget for closing costs. You're responsible for paying your closing costs, not your bank. Don't put every spare penny toward your down payment. Hold back at least 4% of your home's purchase price to be on the safe side.

2 Don't move too often. You'll pay closing costs every time you buy and sell real estate. Moving too often can wipe out any gains from your home going up in value. Try to live in your home at least five years to minimize the closing costs.

3 Calculate your closing costs ahead of time. Don't be blindsided by closing costs. Ask your agent and your lawyer ahead of time for a breakdown of the most common closing costs.

Common Closing Costs and Disbursements

Buyers face several closing costs and disbursements. Which ones you're responsible for paying depends on where you're buying and whether the home is new or resale. Some of those discussed below may apply to you, others may not.

The Home Inspection:
Making Sure Your Home Is a Wise Investment

Cost: $500 (approximately; varies depending on property type)

I strongly encourage you to get a home inspection done before investing your life savings in a single asset (the family home). A home inspection is money well spent. Though no home inspection can find everything, a good one gives you the peace of mind that you've done what you can to avoid buying a money pit.

A good home inspector will examine every nook and cranny of a home to look for any issues, big or small. Faulty wiring, structural issues and landscaping problems can end up costing you thousands of dollars. A home inspection is a good time to start budgeting for maintenance and repair costs. Your inspector will, when possible (weather may be a factor), point out how the roof is holding up or if the furnace is on its last legs. The inspection can even be used as a bargaining chip when negotiating with sellers. If you find a major unexpected issue like an underground oil tank or lead paint, there's nothing stopping you from asking for a reduction in the purchase price. The seller may be willing to knock a few hundred or thousand dollars off so that you don't walk away from the deal.

Modern technology like infrared thermal imaging cameras (a non-invasive way for inspectors to shows you issues you can't see with the naked eye, like air leaks and moisture intrusion) have made home inspections even more thorough these days, but still, they can only go so far. Your inspector doesn't have carte blanche to tear down walls. Although the inspector can check the electrical panel and fuse box, if there's old knob-and-tube wiring hidden inside the walls, it could be missed.

Even if it means taking time off work, it's worth being present at your home inspection. It's a great learning experience, especially for first-time homebuyers, and the perfect time to ask questions. You'll learn about the inner workings of the home, such as where the water and gas shut-off valves are.

Although inspections are generally thorough, they don't cover everything. That's why I recommend you do your own mini-inspection. Turn on all the faucets, test electrical switches and make sure appliances work—preheat the oven; turn on the dishwasher, washer and dryer. This can help avoid any costly surprise repair bills after your move-in date.

Sometimes a home inspection isn't enough. If you're buying in an area prone to termites, consider bringing in a termite inspector to be on the safe side. Likewise, if you find mould, a mould inspection and air-quality testing are worthwhile.

You may be wondering whether an inspection on a new home is needed. The answer is yes. Although you'll get a walk-through with your builder before you move in, it's still worthwhile to hire an independent inspector who specializes in new homes. An inspector can make sure your new home is move-in ready. They may come across deficiencies overlooked by the builder and municipal inspectors (e.g., the appliances may not be properly hooked up). You can file a claim under the builder's warranty and (hopefully) have it remedied before your move-in date.

Review Municipality Records

Before buying a home, request a copy of its records from city hall. This will give you a heads-up about any issues the seller may have failed to disclose, such as the roots from a nearby tree breaking into the drain pipes, and what measures were taken.

Likewise, it's worthwhile to get an inspection done when buying a condo—new or resale. Although obviously you won't be solely responsible for costly repairs like a new roof or windows, there are other things that can go wrong. Hire an inspector familiar with condos. An inspection will typically cover the major components of your condo, including electrical, HVAC, plumbing and the common elements.

Hiring an Expert Home Inspector

You really need to do your homework when hiring an inspector. The home-inspection industry is by and large unregulated in Canada. In some provinces, all you need is to pass a weekend course and you can call yourself a home inspector. Here are three tips for hiring one:

- **Find the right inspector.** Ask family and friends who have recently bought a home for recommendations. You can also find lists of inspectors on industry websites, including the Canadian Association of Home and Property Inspectors (cahpi.ca). You might think twice before taking a recommendation for an inspector from your agent. Chances are they'll recommend a decent inspector, but there's a clear conflict of interest.

- **Check their certification and experience.** Before hiring an inspector, ask about their certification and experience. Ideally, the home inspector is certified with years of experience in the trades, as a builder or as a city inspector.

- **Select a home inspector** *before* **house hunting.** You never know when you'll find your dream home. Interview at least three inspectors. Choose one, and have another as backup in case your first choice is busy when you see a property you like and are ready to make an offer.

The Real Estate Lawyer: The Unsung Hero in Home Buying

Cost: $1,500 (approximate; varies)

Your lawyer is the unsung hero in the home-buying process, doing all the hard work that goes on behind the scenes. The lawyer will review your offer and the status certificate (if you're buying a condo), ensure the home's title is clear from defects and liens, purchase title insurance, register the home in your name, prepare the statement of adjustments (more on this below), calculate the land transfer taxes, prepare the mortgage paperwork and, finally, give you the keys to your new home.

Lawyers don't come cheap but are worth every penny. Be sure to ask your lawyer for a quote in writing (this includes their fees, plus an estimate of disbursements). When your home closes, compare the final invoice to your quote. If you notice any differences, don't be shy to speak up.

When I noticed the fees on my invoice were higher than the price the lawyer had told me (I was overcharged on the statement of adjustments and for the title search), I mentioned this to him. He refunded me about $500. This is money I put straight toward my mortgage.

Hiring an Expert Real Estate Lawyer

Just as with a home inspector, it's a good idea to start looking for a lawyer *before* you start house hunting. Consider these tips:

- **Referrals:** Ask family and friends for referrals, and search online and in the Yellow Pages. Interview two to three lawyers.

- **Specialties:** Real estate is complex—seek out lawyers who specialize in real estate, not, say, family law. Home buying often moves at a breakneck pace, so make sure they are in good standing and readily available to answer questions.

- **References:** Ask for references of satisfied clients. Take the time to call them.

Land Transfer Tax: The Government's Piece of the Pie

Cost: Varies by province and municipality; typically a percentage of purchase price

Many provinces impose a land transfer tax on home purchases—typically a percentage of the home's purchase price, though some provinces have flat fees. Depending on where you're buying, land transfer tax may be your most expensive closing cost.

To help keep real estate affordable for "property virgins," many provinces offer rebates for first-time homebuyers. In Toronto, homebuyers are hit with a double whammy of land transfer taxes: a provincial tax and a municipal tax. If you bought an $800,000 home in Toronto, you'd pay provincial land transfer tax of $12,475 and municipal land transfer tax of $11,725, for a grand total of $24,200. If you are a first-time homebuyer, with rebates you'd pay slightly less, $16,475.

Want to calculate your land transfer taxes? RateHub.ca has a helpful calculator.

Other Closing Costs Not to Overlook

Your inspector and lawyer fees aren't the only closing costs you'll have to contend with. Here are other closing costs you may face:

- **Title insurance:** Bought through your lawyer, title insurance protects your property's title from property tax owing, liens, rights of way and unpaid work orders, among other things. Most lenders require you to purchase title insurance before approving your mortgage (approximate cost: $100 to $300).

- **Appraisal fee:** An appraisal confirms that the value of the properly is in line with the purchase price. If you're lucky, your lender may foot the bill (approximate cost: $250 to $350).

- **Mortgage insurance:** If you choose to spread the cost of mortgage insurance over the life of your mortgage, like most homebuyers do, it won't be a closing cost per se. However, if you're buying a home in Manitoba, Ontario or Quebec, you'll have to pay the PST on your mortgage insurance on closing day. For example, if you're buying a home in Ontario and your mortgage insurance premium is $8,100, you'll owe $648 on closing (8% PST).

- **Property tax and utility adjustments:** Depending on the billing cycle, sellers may pay utility bills and property tax in advance. As the buyer, you'll need to reimburse the seller for your portion on and after the closing date. Don't worry, you don't need to figure this out yourself—this is taken care of by your lawyer, who will draw up a statement of adjustments.

- **Development and education levies, and utility hookups:** Development and education levies pay for infrastructure like new roads, sewers and schools. Utilities—electricity, heating, water and the like—often charge hookup fees.

- **Changing the locks:** You'll want to hire a locksmith to change the locks.

- **Cleaning:** Although the home being in "broom-swept" condition should be part of the offer, you'll still want to clean it thoroughly before moving in.

- **Appliances:** If the home doesn't come with appliances, you'll have to spring for them. Besides the price tag, appliances may come with delivery and installation charges.

- **Cosmetic updates and renovations:** When you move in, you may want to do renos such as repainting and updates such as changing light fixtures. If the home is a fixer upper and in desperate need of repair, you may choose to undertake major renovations—new roof or windows— right away (for one way to pay for these renos, see the discussion of HELOCs in chapter 11).

- **Equipment and tools:** When you own a home, the landlord is no longer a phone call away. Don't forget to buy tools like a hammer and screwdriver for minor repairs, if you don't already have them. If you have a green thumb, you may want gardening tools. Depending on where you live, you might also need a snow shovel.

Get a Property Survey

Although title insurance is helpful for protecting your property's rights of way, it's a good idea too to have a survey done, especially if you want to build an addition or add a deck, say. You don't want to build on your neighbour's lot by accident! Most properties have been surveyed, so check with your lawyer. If a survey doesn't exist, you'll need to pay for one. To find a licensed surveyor, check your local business directory or Google *land surveyors.*

How the Closing Process Works

Before you move into your new home, you'll need to complete the closing process. Homes typically close in 30 to 120 days. As a buyer, you usually get three walk-throughs before your move-in date (this is included in your offer to purchase). If you were like me, there was a lot going on and you were under a lot of pressure when you first saw the property. Walk-throughs allow you to take a closer look at the property at your leisure. You can take measurements for any furniture you're bringing with you or planning to purchase, and start to plan renos. You'll also want to make sure chattels and light fixtures aren't being swapped out for cheaper models and fixtures. (If chattels and fixtures have been swapped out when you move in, speak with your lawyer.)

Before your closing date, you'll need to pay for some of the closing costs mentioned above, like an inspection and appraisal. A week or so before your closing date, you'll meet with your lawyer to go over the final details and sign the mortgage paperwork. Before your closing date, you'll deliver a certified cheque for your down payment to your lawyer. Once the deed is registered in your name, your lawyer will call you to confirm everything went through and arrange to give you the keys to the new home. Time to throw the confetti! Congratulations, you can finally call yourself a homeowner.

Hiring Movers vs. DIY Moving

The home-buying marathon is almost over. The only thing ahead of you now is the final sprint toward the finish line—aka moving day.

Your final big decision will be whether to do it yourself or hire movers. If you're moving from an apartment and don't have many belongings, DIY may be the way to go. But don't underestimate how much work moving will be. Consider the following when deciding between hiring movers and DIY:

- **How much stuff are you moving?** If you're moving from a house to an even bigger house, you may be better off with movers, since you'll typically have a lot more stuff to move.

- **How far are you moving?** If you're moving just down the street, DIY may be the way to go, but if you're moving to another city, movers may be your best bet.

- **How physically fit are you?** If your idea of exercise is getting up off the couch to grab the remote control, it's probably best to hire movers.

- **Is anyone willing to lend a helping hand?** If none of your family and friends is free to help out, you're probably best to hire a moving company.

If you do decide to go the DIY route, moving can be as simple as renting a U-Haul truck and buying your family and friends beer and pizza for helping out. But note that driving trucks like U-Hauls can be tricky. Call your auto insurance company ahead of time to see if you're covered in the event of an accident. If you're not, buy insurance from the truck rental company. The last thing you want is to get in an accident on moving day and have to pay damages out of pocket. If you're moving to a condo, be sure to book the elevator in advance.

Whether you decide to hire movers or DIY, you'll likely take care of the packing yourself (unless you hire packers, but that costs extra moolah). To avoid stress, don't leave packing until the last minute. Start well in advance—crack open a champagne bottle once your offer is accepted and then begin packing. Start by decluttering. If you haven't used something in a year, it may be time to get rid of it. To help pay for your move, sell some of your stuff on Kijiji or Craigslist, or have a yard sale. Anything of value left over, give to family and friends or donate to charity.

Once you've pared down the clutter, the real fun begins. But before you start packing, make sure you have the essential supplies: boxes, packing tape and a black marker to label boxes. Looking to save money here? Supermarkets and liquor stores are a great source of free boxes—just make sure they're quality ones. You don't want the bottom to break, sending your mother's irreplaceable dishware that has been passed down from generation to generation smashing onto the pavement.

Here are other packing tips to make your move easier:

- Wrap glasses individually with packing paper. Wrap plates with bubble wrap (or clothing to save even more money on supplies) and stack them vertically in boxes, placing scrunched-up packing paper at the top and bottom for added protection.

- To avoid frustration when unpacking and setting up, label the cords on electronics like your computer, Blu-ray player and TV, or better yet, take a photo of the connections before unplugging and packing them up.

- Don't pack unnecessarily. Packing your clothes can be as simple as removing dresser drawers. A huge time-saver is a wardrobe box, to which you just transfer your clothes, still on their hangers. They're available through moving companies and moving-supply stores.

- To make unpacking easier, label boxes by room and content (e.g., *kitchen—dishes*), and whether the contents are fragile. Have the movers or your helpers deposit each box in the room it belongs in.

- Move valuable belongings such as jewellery and personal documents (legal documents, birth certificate, passport, chequebook) yourself.

- If you're anything like me, you'll be dead tired after the move. Pack an overnight bag with all the essentials (clothes, toiletries), so you don't have to unpack the night of the move.

Six Tips for Hiring Honest Movers

Most movers are honest, but there are horror stories that will keep you up at night. CBC's *Marketplace* did an episode called "Movin' Day Showdown" about dishonest movers. The moving industry has been described as the Wild West. Unscrupulous movers are doing everything from overcharging customers to holding their belongings ransom. If you decide to hire movers, make sure you do your homework:

1 Consider only those movers who take the time to come see what's to be moved before giving you a quote.

2 Get at least three written quotes. Make sure the quote is part of your contract. This will cover your derrière if the movers decide to overcharge you.

3 To avoid the bad apples, check with family, friends and colleagues.

4 Check on the Better Business Bureau website for customer complaints.

5 If you have home insurance, check with your provider whether you're covered for moving and, if so, what the deductible is. Also ask the movers if they're insured, should anything be damaged during your move. You'll want to consider buying replacement value protection, which means the movers are legally liable up to the estimate of the value of your belongings being moved. Ask for the name of the mover's insurance provider and

their policy number. Find out if there's a deductible you'd have to pay and how much. For more on hiring movers, see the federal Office of Consumer Affairs' informative webpage "The Consumer Checklist for Choosing a Moving Company."

6   Make sure the moving contract covers who is responsible if any of your belongings are lost or damaged, or if the floors or doors of the home you're moving from or into are damaged.

Furnish Your Home for Less

A major expense many of us forget about is furniture. When my parents moved into their first home, they used a cardboard box as a coffee table because that's all they could afford. Unless you want to come home to an empty home for the first few months, start thinking about furniture before you move. You'll also need bedding, kitchenware, tableware and the like.

If you're moving from one home to another, you likely already have some furnishings. Don't get too caught up over style. The only one who will notice the clashing drapes and couch is you. Remember to take measurements to make sure your furniture fits your new home.

Family members might have furniture they're happy to part with. This is a good start, but you'll often need more. Here are good places to get decent furnishing for less:

- **Online:** Websites like Craigslist and Kijiji are great for finding furniture at a discount. Sellers may even drop the furniture off at your home if you don't have a vehicle.

- **Garage sales:** One person's trash is another person's treasure. Go to sales early before all the good items are gone.

- **Thrift stores:** You may find a diamond in the rough at a thrift store. Look for dents, scratches or other imperfections on furniture. Figure out whether you can repair it or learn to live with it.

- **Ikea:** Ikea is Swedish for "save a bundle." The assembly instructions aren't always easy to follow, so set aside an afternoon—or day—to build your furniture.

- **Discount stores:** There are often great deals to be had at stores like HomeSense on bedding, kitchenware, small furniture pieces, and home decorations.

- **Gifts:** For holidays, birthdays and housewarming parties, mention to family and friends that you'd really appreciate something for your new home. It doesn't have to be furniture. Bedding, dinnerware and linens are other items you may need—or a gift card to a store of your choice.

* * * * *

5 Key Mortgage-Burning Takeaways

➤ **Budget for closing costs and disbursements.** Earmark 1.5% to 4% of your home's purchase price for closing costs.

➤ **Look for an inspector and lawyer early on.** Don't wait until you're ready to make an offer to find them. Interview two to three.

➤ **Decide to hire movers or DIY.** Figure out how much stuff you'll be moving. If you decide to hire movers, do your homework to hire honest ones.

➤ **Plan ahead for packing.** Leave yourself plenty of time to pack. To make unpacking easier, label boxes clearly.

➤ **Be on the lookout for furniture at a bargain.** Ask family and friends for any furniture they don't need. Frequent garage sales, look for bargains on Craigslist and Kijiji, frequent off-price stores and Ikea.

Part 3

Congratulations, You're a Homeowner! Now What?

There are worse things in life than death.
Have you ever spent an evening with an insurance salesman?
WOODY ALLEN

13
Protecting Your Castle
Emergency Funds, Insurance, Prenups and Wills

YOU'RE A PROUD homeowner. You're on top of the world. Then disaster strikes. You lose your job, you get divorced or your home is damaged in a storm (or all the above. Yikes!). To make sure all your bases are covered, you'll want to take steps to protect your home.

In this chapter we look at ways to prepare for what I call "home-owner Armageddon." We go over the importance of an emergency fund, ways to protect your home if your marriage is on the rocks and more. As I've said, your home is most likely your family's most valuable asset. Start treating it that way by giving it the attention it deserves.

Saving for a Rainy Day: Why You Need an Emergency Fund

Are you prepared for a financial emergency? Whether you lose your job, your water pipe bursts or your roof starts leaking, it's important to have a backup plan. Many people use their line of credit—or, worse, their credit card—for unforeseen expenses, but this can prove costly.

In the second summer as a homeowner, I spent over $25,000 on home repairs. How did I pay for this without going into debt? With my emergency fund. Financial experts recommend socking away three to six months' living expenses in a savings account. Personally, I like to keep things simple. I make sure I always have $10,000 sitting in my savings account. It gives me peace of mind knowing I won't be caught off guard by unexpected expenses.

When Not to Save Up a Big Emergency Fund

For most people, it makes sense to have a sizable emergency fund, but sometimes it doesn't. If you have credit card debt, for example, you're better off focusing on paying that off first.

Don't make the mistake of putting every spare penny toward your down payment and closing costs. Hold back some money for your emergency fund. I know that $10,000 is a lot to save, especially if you're making the minimum down payment. So try to save $1,000, $2,000 or whatever you can afford. Once you're settled in your home, work on building your emergency fund.

Home Insurance: Safeguarding Your Worldly Possessions

Cost: Varies depending on several factors, including your home's value, its content, and the perceived risk

Buying a home is a busy time. You'll want to leave yourself plenty of time to buy home insurance. Not only is it required by most lenders, you'll want it in place to protect your home and everything inside. There are three main types:

- **Basic:** Your no-frills insurance policy. It protects your home only from named perils, such as fire, hail, windstorms and vandalism.

- **Broad:** Falls in the middle of the insurance continuum. It costs more than basic but provides further protection from extra hazards named in your policy.

- **Comprehensive:** Provides the highest level of protection but costs the most. It protects your home and its contents from all risks except those named in your policy. Things like flooding and wear and tear are typically excluded.

All insurance policies aren't created equal. When shopping for home insurance, make sure you're comparing apples to apples. Read the fine print so you understand what you're signing up for.

Six Simple Ways to Save on Home Insurance

Looking to save on home insurance? You're not alone. Home insurance premiums have been skyrocketing in recent years because of extreme weather events, so don't be shocked to see yours jump when it's time to renew. But don't despair. Although an insurance premium is a small price to pay to protect your most valuable asset, your home, here are simple ways to save:

1 **Shop around.** Get a few quotes from insurance companies and brokers. Websites like Kanetix.ca help make it easy to shop for the best home insurance rate. Consider using an insurance agent or broker to shop the market and find the insurance policy that best meets your needs.

2 **Raise your deductible.** Your deductible is the amount you pay out of pocket when filing a claim with your provider. You probably wouldn't make a claim for $500 (since it could cause your premium to rise), so consider raising your deductible to $1,000 or $2,000 to lower your premium (just make sure you have enough money in your emergency fund to cover unexpected expenses).

Keep Your Insurance Company in the Loop
Be sure to let your home insurance company know your plans before doing any major renovations or renting to tenants. Not doing so can void your insurance policy.

3 **Bundle and save.** Get a discount by taking out home and auto insurance with the same company (just make sure you're getting a good deal on both).

4 **Put safety first.** Many providers offer discounts for installing carbon monoxide and smoke detectors and home alarm systems.

5 **Consider annual versus monthly.** Some companies offer a discount if you pay your premium for the year in a lump sum in advance, instead of monthly.

6 **Look into other discounts.** You may get a discount for paying off your mortgage (yet another reason to be mortgage-free sooner). Take advantage of group rates through your university alumni association or professional association.

Disability Insurance: Protecting Your Ability to Earn a Paycheque

You probably wouldn't think twice about protecting your home or car, but what about your ability to earn a paycheque? Disability insurance is important yet often overlooked. Life insurance helps your family if you pass away; disability insurance helps provide for your family financially so food still gets put on the table and the mortgage still gets paid if you get sick or injured. One in three people will be disabled for 90 days or more at least once in their life before age 65.[1] Although many employers offer disability insurance, it may not be enough.

There are two main types of disability insurance: group and individual. If you work for a company, you're most likely covered by group disability. Some group policies offer only limited coverage—for example, 60% of your take-home pay. If you have group disability, take the time to review your policy to make sure it's sufficient. If it isn't enough, think about getting additional individual disability insurance. Not only will it cover you if you switch jobs, unlike group, most individual policies let you collect benefits even if you're partially disabled.

If you're self-employed, your business is your livelihood, so disability insurance is especially important. Group disability insurance can often be obtained through professional associations. Be sure to look into individual disability policies also.

Life Insurance: Protecting Loved Ones and Your Home

We've come to everyone's favourite part of the book—life insurance (end sarcasm). I know that discussing life insurance is about as much fun as organizing your sock drawer, but it's an important topic that shouldn't be overlooked. If you're a single guy or gal (or the heirs of

Bill Gates), you can probably get by without life insurance. For everyone else, it's important to have life insurance in place, especially when you own an asset like a home and have dependents—spouse, children, elderly parents—living with you. If your family would struggle to pay the mortgage without your paycheque, life insurance is a must.

There are two main types of life insurance: *term* and *permanent* (also called *whole life* or *universal*). Term life provides coverage for a specific period of time—typically 5 to 30 years. Permanent life provides coverage until you pass away or your premiums are unpaid. The premiums are usually higher for permanent than term because they're averaged over your lifetime, whereas the premiums for term are averaged over the length of your coverage only.

For most families, term is the way to go—it provides homeowners with low-cost coverage. I know what you're thinking: term insurance is like rent—you're throwing your money away. You could say that about other types of insurance too. You're not going to go, "Aw shucks, my home didn't burn down, so I paid for home insurance for no reason all those years!"

So, how long should you cover yourself with term life insurance? For families with young children, term 20 is probably the way to go. Your family will be protected until your children are grown up and (hopefully) financially independent. Since quotes for term vary among insurance companies, get a few before deciding which provider to go with.

You might also consider *combination insurance*, which provides life, critical illness (a lump sum if you're diagnosed with a critical illness that's listed in your contract, typically including cancer, heart attack and stroke) and disability insurance in one, in a more cost-effective policy. This type of insurance has various structures when it comes to how you can draw on the benefits, so be sure you understand it before making the switch, and also ensure you're not giving up any coverage you need under your existing policies.

Life insurance can be complicated. Speak with an insurance agent or broker in order to make an informed decision. Then be sure you get around to actually signing up for it. Many people don't, then 10 years down the road they die unexpectedly, without any coverage. If you have dependents, run, don't walk, to sign up for term life insurance.

Mortgage Life Insurance: Protecting the Bank

For most families, a mortgage represents the largest debt of their lifetime. Although mortgage life insurance may look good at first glance, it has shortcomings. The big banks market mortgage life insurance like it's a must-have. Mortgage life insurance is similar to term life insurance. If you were to suddenly die, suffer a terminal illness or be involved in a serious accident, your mortgage would be paid off (usually up to a maximum amount, say $500,000). The banks make it easy to sign up—and make you sign a waiver so you can't hold the bank responsible for a bad turn of events. Once you sign up, the premium is conveniently paid as part of your regular mortgage payments.

Protect Your Family *Before* Moving into Your Home

Arrange to have term life insurance in place before you move into your new home. If you won't be covered in time, sign up for mortgage life insurance for a few months until your term life insurance coverage is in place.

So far, so good, right? But here's where mortgage life insurance starts to take a turn for the worse. The banks boast that you can sign up for it without the hassle of a medical exam. Although that may save time up front, it can prove costly. Here's what the bank isn't telling you: you might not be covered. The bank can deny your claim if it learns you had a pre-existing health condition you weren't aware of or forgot to disclose when you signed up. This is called *post-claims underwriting*. Only when you or your family makes a claim do you learn you're not actually covered.

Another shortcoming of mortgage life insurance is that it's declining coverage. Even though your premium doesn't go up on renewal, you're paying for less coverage as time goes on. The more you pay down your mortgage, the less coverage you're getting. For example, if you have a $500,000 mortgage, you're initially covered for $500,000 by mortgage life insurance, but if in 10 years you only have $200,000 left on your mortgage, you're covered for only $200,000 (if you had a term policy for $500,000, your coverage wouldn't decline during its term).

Mortgage Life Insurance vs. Term Life Insurance

Instead of mortgage life insurance, a far better choice for families with dependents is term life insurance. The premiums of term life and mortgage life insurances are comparable, but term life insurance is a lot more flexible. With term life insurance, you can pay off your mortgage, cover your funeral and help pay for your children's college. With mortgage life insurance, you can only pay off your mortgage. What your bank isn't telling you is that with mortgage life insurance, you're paying for an insurance policy with your bank—instead of your loved ones—as the beneficiary.

Protecting Your Ass(ets): The Cohabitation Agreement and Prenup

I'm all for storybook endings, but divorce is an unfortunate part of life for many people these days. Forty-one percent of marriages end in divorce before the 30th year.[2] The top cause? Money.

I bet former Beatle Paul McCartney wishes he had signed a prenup. He paid out almost $50 million in a divorce settlement to his second wife Heather Mills (hopefully he learned his lesson and signed a prenup with his third wife).

I hope your relationship or marriage works out and you're together for the years to come, but it's important to be prepared in case it doesn't.

The Matrimonial Home

When it comes to the family home (referred to in law as the *matrimonial home*), it's important to recognize there's a difference between living common law and being married. Family law differs depending on where you live, so I'll discuss it only in general terms here.

Let's say that prior to their relationship, Kanye owns a home and Kim doesn't. With their relationship going well, Kanye invites Kim to move in. Fast-forward three years and things aren't working out. If the couple were married, Kim would be entitled to half the value of the home, since it's considered the matrimonial home. But if Kanye and

Kim are living common law, Kim would likely only be entitled to half of the home's price increase during the time she lived there (i.e., she wouldn't automatically be entitled to half the home's value).

The above is meant only to serve as a cautionary tale—I'm not a family lawyer, but I recommend consulting with one before moving in together.

Signing a Cohabitation or Prenup Agreement

Whether you're still dating or ready to walk down the aisle, it's important to have "the talk." No, I'm not talking about the birds and the bees, I'm talking about, in the words of Kevin O'Leary, the "only thing that matters in life—money." I wouldn't suggest asking to see your love interest's bank statement on the first date, but you will likely have a general sense of their money habits by the third date.

There's no set time in a relationship to have the money talk, as long as it's before moving in together. Find out about your partner's income—what they own (assets) and what they owe (debts). While it would be nice to simply be able to take your fiancé's word for it, politely ask for proof in writing, like a financial statement. (Hey, the bank wouldn't get into a relationship with you without seeing proof, and you shouldn't either.)

Time It Right

Asking your partner to sign a cohabitation or pre-nup agreement is all about timing. There's a right way to do it and a wrong way. (You'll find lots of advice about it from relationship experts online.)

There's often a difference between perception and reality. Your fiancé might drive a BMW and wine and dine you at fancy restaurants, but when you look at his finances, you could find out he owns nothing and owes everyone. I'm not saying to throw him under the bus and end your relationship right then and there. This is the perfect opportunity to work together as a couple to overcome the challenges, building a financial foundation and future.

If you're ready to move in together, it's time to put your love in writing. A cohabitation agreement is a written contract spelling out the rights and responsibilities of the unmarried couple in case the relationship ends. A prenuptial agreement is similar but for couples who are getting married.

Most couples benefit from a cohabitation or prenup agreement, but it may not make sense for everyone. (The scene in a *Seinfeld* episode where George Costanza asks his fiancée to sign a prenup and she bursts out laughing because he doesn't have any money comes to mind.) If you're 20-somethings who don't own anything and are renting together, you can probably skip the cohabitation agreement (though it wouldn't hurt to speak with a lawyer about it first).

Wills

There are two things certain in life: death and taxes. I know, talking about wills is about as fun as getting a root canal without freezing, but it's one of those necessary evils (like filing your taxes). A will is a must-have for anyone with a spouse, child, dependant or major asset (ahem, a home). But the sad reality is that many people don't have a will when they pass away. Pop superstar Prince died without a will; he's not alone. Over half of Canadians don't have a signed will.[3]

So what are the consequences of dying without a will? If you die intestate (which is a fancy word for "without a will"), your province of residence will decide how your property is to be divided and who will look after your kids. You may want to give your home to your spouse, but without a will, your assets will be divided according to the law. Do you really want to leave an important decision like this in the hands of your province? If not, a will is the way to go.

Although a lot of people know the importance of having a will, they never get around to preparing one. A will is one of those things to make time for. Your family will already be grief-stricken by your death—do you really want to add the complication of your dying without a will? Having a will drawn up is money well spent. It can actually help your heirs save money. If you die intestate, it will take your heirs a lot more time and money to obtain probate (a fancy word for "establishing the validity of the will"), not to mention the fighting it can cause. Do you want to be remembered with fondness, or for the turmoil you caused for dying without a will?

So you know you need a will. Now what? There are two options: you can go to a lawyer, or draft up your own will with a do-it-yourself kit. I suggest that you have a lawyer prepare your will. A lawyer will draft your will to ensure it holds up in court. Preparing your will with software can be a case of penny wise, pound foolish. Unless you have a cookie-cutter estate, it's best to have a lawyer draft it up. If you do decide to prepare your own will, at least have a lawyer review it.

Your will isn't written in stone. Make a habit of reviewing it every year or two. You'll want to update it after major life events (e.g., getting married or the birth of your child), or if you purchase a major asset like a home, rental property or car.

Joint Tenants vs. Tenants in Common

When you're buying property with someone else, you can own it in one of two ways: as joint tenants or as tenants in common.

With property owned by *joint tenants*, when one tenant dies, the property belongs to the surviving tenant (called *right of survivorship*). This arrangement is most common among married couples. Let's say Kate Capshaw and Steven Spielberg own a luxurious cottage in the beautiful Muskoka region of Ontario, and that, sadly, Steven passes away. Even though Steven had wanted to leave his share of the cottage to his kids from his first marriage, he couldn't, since he was a joint tenant. But now that Kate owns the property on her own, she can leave it to her kids from her first marriage (Hollywood marriages are messy), while Steven's kids potentially get nothing.

However, if Steven and Kate had owned the cottage as *tenants in common*, Steven could have willed his share of the cottage to his kids. This is because, with property owned by tenants in common, each person owns a share of the property, and each tenant can will their share to whomever they want. Which means that when one tenant dies, unlike with joint tenancy, the property doesn't automatically pass to the other tenant. A tenants-in-common arrangement is most common in second marriages or when buying a property with someone who isn't your spouse—for example, a sibling or friend.

With blended families being common today, the decision of tenancy is more important than ever. Speak to your lawyer and whomever you're buying the property with, and choose the ownership structure that makes the most sense.

Power of Attorney and Living Will

Besides a will, it's also important to have a power of attorney and living will. A power of attorney is a document that appoints someone you trust to make medical and financial decisions on your behalf when you're not able to. For example, if you're in a coma after a car accident, a *power of attorney* will help ensure your mortgage payments get made, so you don't lose your home. A *living will* specifies your wishes if you're on life support. If you want to be kept alive at all costs, your home may have to be sold to pay for your medical care.

• • • • •

5 Key Mortgage-Burning Takeaways

➤ **Protect your home with insurance.** Protect your most valuable asset, your home. Home insurance comes in three main types: basic, broad and comprehensive.

➤ **Get disability insurance.** Disability insurance can help pay the mortgage if you get sick or injured. Review your group policy at work to make sure the coverage is sufficient. Consider an individual policy if you're self-employed.

➤ **Cover yourself with life insurance.** If you have a family, life insurance is a must. It can help pay off the mortgage if you suddenly die. Term life insurance is an affordable option for homeowners.

➤ **Sign a cohabitation or prenup agreement.** To avoid any nasty surprises, sign a cohabitation or prenup agreement. Outline what happens to major assets like your home if your relationship doesn't work out.

➤ **Prepare a will.** Death is a fact of life. Specify in your will who you want your home to go to. Prepare a power of attorney and living will so your mortgage will continue to be paid when you're not able to take care of your financial affairs.

Your task is not to foresee the future but to enable it.
ANTOINE DE SAINT-EXUPÉRY, poet

14

Turning Your Home into an Income Source
Becoming a Landlord

YOU OWN YOUR dream home and you've taken the steps to protect it—life is pretty good—but you still have a massive mortgage hanging over your head.

Becoming a landlord is one of the easiest ways to burn your mortgage sooner. With a secondary suite such as a basement apartment, you can turn your home into an income-producing asset. By renting part of it out, you're unlocking its true potential. Once your mortgage is paid off, you can keep renting and building your net worth, if you wish. Simply put, a rental property is the ultimate solution to building long-term wealth and achieving financial freedom. As homeowner, through creative living arrangements like living in your home's basement and renting out the upstairs, or sharing your condo with roommates, you can pay down your mortgage even sooner.

If you're anything like me, one of your biggest fears as a homeowner is losing your job and not being able to pay the mortgage. Jobs are far from certain these days. Tenants act as safety nets and can help you carry your home if you're unexpectedly laid off.

A lot of home TV shows like to focus on the sexier side of real estate: house flipping. House flipping can be a good way to make a quick buck, but it's also a good way to lose your shirt. Rental properties—that is, the slow and steady approach—are where the real money's at. Scott McGillivray of *Income Property* is living proof. He was my inspiration for becoming a landlord. McGillivray started with a single student rental property; today he owns over a hundred rental properties.

Ready to become a landlord? In this chapter we'll look at things to consider when renting out your property. We'll also look at ways to land a dream tenant and avoid the nightmare ones.

So You Think You Want to Be a Landlord

A rental property can be a cash cow, but it also comes with a lot of responsibilities, and the decision to become a landlord isn't one to be taken lightly. Make sure you're cut out for it before taking the plunge. Here are things to consider about being a landlord before renting out your place:

Pros

- **Paying off your mortgage in about half the time:** The extra income generated is why most people decide to become landlords. The rent earned can be used to cover your home's monthly expenses. You can make mortgage lump-sum payments with the money left over.

- **Building a nest egg:** Once you're mortgage-free, why stop renting? Start savings toward your next goals, like early retirement or buying a standalone rental property.

- **Being the boss:** Owning a rental property is like owning your own business—and you're in charge! You get to make all the important decisions—setting the rent, marketing your property and choosing the tenants.

- **Claiming tax deductions:** Rental income must be reported on your tax return. To help reduce your tax bill, deduct expenses related to your rental property, including mortgage interest, home insurance, property tax and utilities.

- **Creating your own safety net:** A tenant acts as a safety net—the rent is like an extra paycheque coming in. It's the perfect way to supplement your income during maternity or paternity leave, or your severance pay after a job loss. Tenants also help reduce the stress of being a first-time homebuyer and carrying a home on your own.

Cons

- **Sharing your personal space:** Although you won't be living in the same unit together, you may be sharing common areas, such as the yard and laundry room. Make sure you're comfortable with just having other people in the house. It can be disruptive if your tenants are having guests over at all hours of the day and playing loud music with bass. If you're a single female homeowner, will you be comfortable renting to male tenants?

Earning Sweat Equity

Are you handy around the house? Roll up your sleeves and earn yourself some sweat equity. Renos and upgrades like refacing kitchen cabinets and installing a dishwasher can boost your rental income potential and property's value.

- **Handling tenants:** Tenants aren't a guaranteed income source. Your tenant can stop paying their rent at any time, leaving you to carry your home on your own. Tenants have many rights. You can't just pack up your tenant's belongings and evict them, but there are ways to protect yourself (more on this later).

- **Dealing with emergencies:** When you're a landlord, be prepared to be on call 24/7. There's never a good time for a flooding basement or gas leak, but if it happens at 3 a.m., you have to be ready to deal with it.

- **Facing higher maintenance and repair costs:** Although there are plenty of excellent tenants out there, renters tend to not take the same pride of ownership as homeowners. Be ready to spend more on maintenance and repairs. You'll want to keep your property in good shape to attract top dollar from renters and for when you sell one day. (And for your own enjoyment too!)

Why I Chose to Live in the Basement and Rent Out the Upstairs

Even before I bought my house, I wanted to be a landlord, but I never imagined living in the basement and renting out the upstairs. Instead, I planned to do the opposite, as most homeowners who have a basement suite do. Then I watched *Income Property* and an idea came to me: to own a home and pay it off sooner, I'd follow in the footsteps of the host Scott McGillivray.* He lived in the basement and rented out the upstairs of his first house for nine years, to get ahead financially.

Once I did the math, it was an easy decision. Would I rather live upstairs and rent out the basement, making $800 a month, or vice versa, and make about twice as much, $1,600? To borrow a line from McGillivray, I went with option two. It just didn't make sense to live upstairs on my own in a spacious three-bedroom, two-bathroom home. Besides the fact that I'm rarely at home, a bigger living space meant more furniture to buy and more space to keep clean. If you've never lived in the basement before, it can take some getting used to, but if you choose respectful tenants (who won't make a racket upstairs) and take steps to reduce noise, it can be well worth it.

I'm the first to admit that living in the basement isn't practical or suitable for everyone. If you're single or a couple, you may be able to swing it, but if you have kids, you'll probably want to live upstairs and rent out the basement. Remember, living in the basement and renting out the upstairs doesn't have to be forever. You can try out it and see how you like it. If you don't like it, you can always move upstairs and rent out the basement instead. Choose the living arrangement that works best for you.

Roommate Rather Than Tenant

It would be nice to be able to afford a spacious detached house with a secondary suite, but for many people buying in big cities, that's just not realistic. A lot of first-time homebuyers are choosing condos over

---

* In case you've never tuned in, *Income Property* is a show about homeowners who renovate their properties to bring in extra rental income and boost their home's value. It's a must-watch for anyone serious about becoming a landlord.

houses. Not only are condos usually more affordable, but some people prefer the condo lifestyle over the added responsibilities that come with owning a house.

Earning rental income with a condo is different from earning it from a house. With a house you can rent out the basement or turn it into a duplex. You can't do that with a condo, but that doesn't mean you can't bring in extra income. Having roommates can be a good way to subsidize your mortgage, as long as you're comfortable sharing your personal space with someone.

Soundproofing Your Home for Less
Resilient channels and Roxul insulation can help dramatically cut down on ambient noise, but they don't come cheap. Twenty dollars' worth of door sweeps and foam tape, though, will go a long way toward reducing it. Install on the interior doors separating the basement and upstairs. These alone won't cut all the noise, but you'll be less likely to hear others' conversations and be able to enjoy some well-deserved peace and quiet.

Since you'll be sharing accommodations, find a roommate suited to your lifestyle. (If you prefer quiet activities like reading or working on the computer, and your roommate likes to crank up the music and party, this is a recipe for disaster.) Some condos come with rental restrictions, so check the rules *before* renting out.

Roommates aren't just for condos. If your house or townhouse doesn't have a secondary suite, roommates might be a good option: you'll split the bills, making homeownership more affordable. If you're not ready to become a full-time landlord, earn some extra cash by renting out your place on short-term rental websites like Airbnb (see the appendix).

Signing the Lease

Whether you have a roommate or tenant, it's important to make it official by putting your rental agreement in writing with a lease. The lease specifies important details, including the names of the landlord and tenant, address of the property, rent amount and when it's due (e.g., the first of the month), length of the lease (usually one year), the notice period for terminating the lease, responsibilities for household chores (snow shovelling, mowing the lawn) and restrictions on guests, pets and smoking, to name a few.

Attracting the Perfect Tenant

Before you can bring in rental income, you'll need to find a tenant. Here are my top tips for attracting the perfect tenant.

Pricing the Rental Unit

Just like when you're selling your home, it's important to price your rental unit properly. Pricing your rental unit too high could mean attracting a smaller pool of tenants and possibly losing a month's rent. You're much better off charging rent at or slightly below fair market value to attract more tenants.

Before you decide on the rent, take the time to look at similar rentals in your neighbourhood. Find out how much rent is being charged and what perks are being offered, for example, free cable and Internet. If your property is up for rent and you haven't had many showings (perhaps you've done a poor job of advertising it), phone people who viewed your property for feedback, and tweak your rental ad as needed.

Protecting Your Landlord Self

Although plenty of free leases are available online, you're better off contacting your real estate lawyer or a local rental association for a lease. With a well-written lease, your best interests are covered as a landlord. Consider making it a condition of the lease that your tenants must get renter's insurance (aka tenant's insurance). Not only will this protect your tenants' possessions, but your insurance provider may give you a discount.

Structuring the Rent: Inclusive or Plus Utilities?

An important decision for landlords is whether to make the rent inclusive or plus utilities. This can mean the difference between earning a profit and losing money. Rent that is inclusive is typically a higher amount than rent plus utilities, since utilities are included. Conversely, rent plus utilities is typically lower than inclusive rent, since the tenant is paying a share of the utility costs (though the amount should be about equal to rent that is inclusive once utilities are included). The three main utilities for homeowners are electricity, water and heat. As a landlord, you usually control heating (provided there isn't a separate thermostat in the rental suite), but you're at the mercy of your tenant for electricity and water.

The decision between inclusive and plus utilities comes down to which arrangement you feel most comfortable with (and you'll need to figure this out *before* you advertise the suite). With my first two sets of tenants, I went with inclusive. This worked fine with the first set, but not so great for the second. Since the second set of tenants wasn't paying a share of utilities, they didn't pay attention to how much electricity they used. In fact, they left on a space heater for two months straight (even when they weren't home!). Not only did this cause my monthly electricity bill to double from $100 to $200, it was a potential fire hazard.

For my third set of tenants, I switched to plus utilities. My tenants are responsible for 60% of utilities. I calculate their portion, and each month provide them with a photocopy of the utility bills, after blacking out the account number and other sensitive information.

When your tenant pays a share of the utilities, they're more likely to turn off the lights and not use up all the hot water. It's often said that you don't want to raise the rent on good tenants for fear of losing them. When the rent is structured as plus utilities, you don't have to—at least, not because of the cost of the utilities. Utility rates are a major expense for landlords and tend to go up a lot faster than inflation. Since your tenant is still paying the same share, they're helping pay a portion of the increase.

As well, rent plus utilities is a lot more attractive from a marketing perspective. Which sounds better: $1,600 per month, or $1,450 per month plus 60% of utilities? I'm willing to bet the second one.

Advertising the Rental Unit

Advertising is how you let the world know you have posh digs for rent. To attract the best possible tenant, you'll want to come up with a marketing strategy. Decide on the type of tenant you're looking for and advertise where you're most likely to find them. If you're looking for a student, advertise at the local college (ask permission first). If you're looking for professionals, advertise in trade publications and at hospitals.

Online dating and rental websites have more things in common than you may think. People tend to take paid dating websites like

Match.com more seriously than free websites like PlentyOfFish. The same is often true for paid versus free rental websites. When you advertise your property on free websites like Craigslist and Kijiji, you're likely to attract a larger pool of tenants, though you may need to do more rigorous vetting. I've had better success finding tenants on paid rental websites. That being said, I did find my third tenants on Craigslist. You could always advertise on both (just screen applicants from free websites extra carefully). Other places and ways to advertise include libraries, community centres, grocery stores, newspapers, Facebook and word of mouth. You can even post an Apartment for Rent sign on your front lawn: include your phone number and specify "by appointment only" so you and any existing tenants you have aren't being constantly bothered by knocks on the door.

Advertising your property and showing it to prospective tenants is time-consuming. If you're too busy, an agent will be happy to lend you a helping hand (usually for one month's rent). The agent will advertise your property, schedule showings and come up with a shortlist of quality tenants. Do your own due diligence and take the time to meet the prospective tenants. You want to make sure you're a good fit for each other.

Writing a Rental Ad That Works

The rental market is competitive, not just for tenants but for landlords too. Writing a decent rental ad is key to attracting quality tenants. Here are tips to get you started:

- **Take quality photos.** Tenants want to be able to picture themselves in their new place. Take the photos yourself if you're a half-decent photographer, or hire a professional. Keep the photos for the next time you're renting out your place.

- **Know your dream tenant.** You can't discriminate by saying things like "Suits professional couple," but there's nothing stopping you from writing an ad targeted toward your dream tenant. Get inside their mind. If you're targeting professionals, say something like "Steps away from the finest restaurants the city has to offer."

- **Come up with a catchy heading.** What sounds more interesting: "Three-bedroom main floor bungalow for rent" or "Tired of sharing utilities? The spacious main floor is all yours!"?

- **Add humour.** Imagine wading through dozens of rental ads, only to come across one that reads, "Looking for a place with hardwood floors, an eat-in kitchen and wood-burning fireplace? We don't have any of those, but we do have air hockey!" Sign me up!

- **Focus on benefits.** It's important to include details like the rent, number of bedrooms and desired move-in date, but don't make the mistake of making that the focus of your ad. What makes your rental suite stand out from the rest? If it's the breathtaking ocean view, don't be shy to say so in the ad.

Screening Applicants

Although it can be tempting to go with the first rental applicant you get, all it takes is one bad tenant to ruin your cash flow. Take the time to screen potential tenants to make sure they're really the great people they say they are. It's much easier to screen out bad tenants than it is to evict them once they're living in your place. Before I meet any in person, I like to speak to them on the phone. This gives me a better feel for them and whether they're a good fit. I use this opportunity to confirm important details, such as when they'd like to move in, and if they have any pets, smoke and are okay with signing a lease.

When screening, be careful not to discriminate based on, for instance, ethnicity, age, sex or disability. For example, if you learn that a prospective tenant has four kids and you'd prefer no kids, you can express your concern that there may not be enough room to accommodate that many people, but you can't refuse to show them the property just because they have children.

There are a few red flags to watch for when screening tenants. If an applicant is full of excuses on being late on rent (some are actually upfront about this) or their credit score is poor, chances are they aren't going to suddenly change their behaviour and become a model tenant overnight. You may be tempted to give them a second chance but, remember, your rental property is a business. One tenant who applied to rent my upstairs seemed decent both in person and on the rental application form, but when I called her landlord, he told me she always paid her rent late, damaged the property and constantly had overnight guests. If I hadn't taken the time to phone her references, she could have been my problem to deal with. Other red flags include the tenant arriving late or not offering to take off their shoes at the door.

When you're a landlord, you're a lot like a bank, but instead of renting money, you're renting space. Banks are hesitant to rent to someone whose income is not always stable—those who are self-employed, paid by commission, on contract or temporary workers—and perhaps with good reason. Consider the prospective tenant's job stability. Although someone may have every intention of paying rent on time, all it takes is a few bad months and they could easily fall behind. Be on the lookout for stated income that seems too high. Ask for Canada Revenue Agency's notice of assessments from the last two years to confirm the tenant's income.

While homeowners often make paying the mortgage their top financial priority, tenants are willing to put other debts like credit card and lines of credit ahead of their rent, for this simple reason: if their rent is a few days late, it won't affect their credit score. The eviction process is also time-consuming and costly. As a landlord, keep this in mind.

For screening tenants, consider using a standard rental application form. The CMHC has an "application to rent" form you can download and print. Make sure applicants complete the form in full. Look for any gaps in their rental history; this may indicate a less-than-stellar past tenancy.

For any applicant you're interested in renting to, start by phoning their references—and don't just call their current landlord (who may give them a glowing reference just to get rid of them); take the time

Review the Residential Tenancy Act

Each province has a website that outlines its residential tenancy act. Take the time to review it. The act outlines important rules surrounding rent increases, evictions and repairs, among other issues.

to call the applicant's last two or three landlords and current employer. Google the tenant's employer to make sure they're real. If everything seems on the level and the tenant is still interested, it's time to do a credit check. Although a credit check costs about $20, it's a small price to pay compared with the cost of evicting a bad tenant.

Complete the Inspection Report

Once you've chosen your tenant and the lease is signed, it's time to complete the inspection report. This report is similar to a home inspection. It documents the condition of your property *before* your tenant moves in.

You may think the inspection report is a waste of time, but it's not. Since you're not living in the rental unit, it can be easy to later forget what its condition was when your tenant moved in. That's why it's best to get it in writing and have your tenant sign off on it. You may also wish to take photos, especially if the suite has hardwood floors, which can be easily damaged.

Before your tenant moves out, you'll review the inspection report together. If you notice any damage beyond regular wear and tear, you can try to seek compensation.

Respect Your Tenant

Although sometimes it may seem like you're a parent instead of a landlord, it's important to respect your tenant. You want the landlord-tenant relationship to be a good one. As a landlord, you're looking for a tenant who will take good care of your property and pay the rent on time. Meanwhile, a tenant is looking for a landlord who is responsive to requests and respects their privacy. If you're polite and respectful to your tenant, give fair notice before entering the rental suite and provide adequate heat, your tenant is in turn more likely to respect your property and you. This can go a long way in reducing tenant turnover (an expensive inconvenience). To show my gratitude for my tenants being good ones, I give them a bottle of wine at New Year's. A small kindness can go a long way.

Be Ready to Fill the (Income) Gap When Your Tenant Leaves

All tenants—good or bad—leave eventually. If you're using the rent to help pay your mortgage, it's important to plan to fill the income gap once your tenant leaves. (If they signed a year lease, you have some peace of mind knowing you have a tenant for 12 months—unless they hit a rough patch and stop paying the rent or break the lease.)

Once your tenant gives notice, start looking for a new tenant right away. Waiting too long can cause you to miss a month's rent. For example, if your property is available for September 1, you'll want to find a tenant by the end of July or early August at the latest. By the time mid-August rolls around, most tenants will be looking for October 1.

Have a plan B in case you aren't able to rent out the suite right away. Have that emergency fund with three to six month's living expenses in a high-interest savings account. It also helps if you have secondary sources of income—a part-time job where you can ask for more hours, or freelance work you can bump up.

• • • • •

5 Key Mortgage-Burning Takeaways

➤ **Be ready to be a landlord**. Renting a part of your home is a great way to pay down your mortgage in about half the time, but it comes with responsibilities. Make sure you're ready before making your place available for rent.

➤ **Consider creative living arrangements**. Looking to pay down your mortgage even sooner? Have you ever considered living in the basement and renting out the upstairs? If you live in a condo, a roommate is another good way to burn your mortgage sooner.

➤ **Price your rental suite properly**. Price it at fair market value to attract a large pool of tenants. Consider charging separately for utilities—your tenant will be less likely to waste utilities, since they're paying a share.

➤ **Screen prospective tenants**. To find a good tenant and avoid the bad ones, take the time to screen applicants. Phone their current and previous landlords and employers, and do a credit check.

➤ **Plan to fill the income gap**. Once your tenant gives notice, start looking for a new tenant right away. Have an emergency fund of three to six months' living expenses.

Afterword
Achieving Financial Freedom: What's Next?

PAYING OFF MY mortgage has changed my life. It's the single most important step toward financial freedom. I hope that your life will change as well after reading my book. For me, the journey toward financial freedom wasn't easy, but it's been well worth it. You too can enjoy financial freedom if you're willing to make it a priority.

A mortgage-free home opens up a world of possibilities. It makes raising children and retiring early a lot easier. With your home paid off, you can start crossing items off your bucket list and pursuing your passions in life, be it travelling, volunteering, starting a business or writing a book. You can afford to take a pay cut to accept a job you truly enjoy—or leave the workforce altogether. It's completely up to you!

A lot of people have asked me what's next, now that my mortgage is paid off. Am I going to move upstairs from the basement or move to a bigger house? I'm not sure, but one thing's for certain: I'm not going to make any snap decisions. I may do one or all of those things, but in due time. (And in case you're wondering, yes, I still pack my lunch and cycle to work—once frugal, always frugal.)

Celebrate your achievement by burning your mortgage, take some well-deserved time to relax and enjoy life even more. Set your next goal and come up with an action plan to achieve it. The biggest mistake you can make is let your new-found cash flow go toward lifestyle inflation. The money I was paying toward my mortgage I'm now funnelling toward index mutual funds. My next goal is to reach a net worth of $1 million by age 35. After that, I'd like to start my own fintech company, buy some rental properties and retire early. (Well, maybe just reduce my workweek to 40 hours ... baby steps.)

We're almost at the end of the book, so here's a recap of the top 10 lessons:

1 Stay motivated. Set SMART goals and come with an action plan to achieve them. Figure out ways to boost your income and cut your expenses.

2 Avoid lifestyle inflation. Stop trying to keep up with the Kardashians. Live below your means.

3 Enjoy the finer things in life—like a Starbucks coffee or your iPhone— but be smart on the big purchases like a home or car.

4 Look for ways to save on food and transportation, the two most costly expenses for many families after mortgage or rent.

5 Pay yourself first. Avoid the temptation to spend. Make saving automatic via direct deposit or preauthorized transfers to a dedicated saving accounts.

6 Balance your home-buying needs and wants. Make a list of each. Narrow down your needs.

7 Don't buy too much home. Aim for a TDS ratio of 37% or below (up to 42% in high-cost cities).

8 Make paying off your mortgage your top financial priority. Don't take 25 or 30 years to pay it off. Set a mortgage-free date and put your plan into action.

9 Take advantage of mortgage prepayments. Make lump-sum payments with "found" money like bonuses, cash gifts, pay raises and tax refunds.

10 Rent out your home. Pay off your mortgage in about half the time. Screen prospective tenants to avoid the bad ones.

My job is far from done. Indeed, this is only the beginning. Mortgage-burning parties used to be a big moment of celebration. Today they're almost unheard of. That may be because we're a lot more comfortable with debt as a society. I want to change that. I want to make mortgage-burning parties cool again. In today's age of easy credit, paying off a mortgage is a major accomplishment that should be celebrated. A mortgage-burning party is a great way to celebrate a major financial milestone and thank family and friends who stuck by you.

I'd love to hear and help in your journey toward burning your mortgage and figure out ways to burn it faster (I'm a mortgage-burning expert, in case you're wondering). Feel free to invite me to your mortgage-burning party (I'll bring the champagne).

Happy mortgage burning!

Appendix
Side Hustle: Paying Off Your Mortgage Even Sooner

H AVE SOME SPARE time? Why not put it to good use and make some extra money with side hustle? I've earned tens of thousands of dollars in side hustle (more than my full-time job) in the last four years. With the extra money you can save toward a down payment, or if you already own a home, pay it off sooner. Here are creative side hustles:

- **Blogging:** If you're passionate about something, why not earn extra money writing about it? Get paid to write someone else's blog, or start your own and make money through advertising like Google AdSense. Buy a domain name (about $15), find a web host and have your blog up and running for less than $100 a year.

- **Childcare:** Look after other people's kids.

- **Clinical research trials:** If you're healthy, get paid to test out new drugs.

- **Coaching:** Career coach, money coach, sports coach—the possibilities are endless.

- **Computer programming and repairs:** If you're talented at computer programming, set up your own website to advertise your skills, or look for jobs online. Or start your own business repairing other people's computers.

- **Dog walking:** Earn extra money walking Fido. The more dogs, the more money (just watch out for these pesky squirrels or Fluffy, the neighbour's cat).

- **Driving or renting your car:** If you're used to chauffeuring around your family, why not chauffeur around paying customers by joining Uber? If you're too busy to drive others, rent out your car through Turo.

- **Errands:** Websites like AskforTask help connect you with busy people who need a helping hand with errands or basic repairs around the house (think of it as an odd-job matchmaker).

- **Focus groups:** A focus group is similar to an online survey, but it's usually done in person. You're paid to express your opinion on a product or service. You can earn about $50 for a one-hour session. You can sign up online.

- **Home restaurant:** Do you have a passion for cooking? Why not start a home restaurant? Websites like Feastly and EatWith help connect you with customers looking for a unique dining experience at an affordable price. Don't want guests in your home? MealSurfers and similar websites let home cooks sell food for pickup.

- **Home-based business:** If you have a good idea and the entrepreneurial spirit, start your own business. The best businesses are often those with low start-up costs (just whatever you do, don't take out a second mortgage on your home).

- **Housesitting:** Look after someone's house while they're away.

- **Parking space rental:** If you don't own a car, rent out your parking place at your condo (just make sure you aren't breaking any rules).

- **Part-time job:** I know what you're thinking. Retail, yuck! But there are a lot more jobs than those at the mall. Bank telling, bartending and working at a clothing store (make sure you get a store discount!) are all good ways to earn money.

- **Photography:** If you're a skilled photographer, take photos at special events like weddings and graduations.

- **Plasma donation:** Donate plasma to help save lives—and get paid for it (about $25 per donation).

- **Renting out your home for filming:** Rent out your home while you're at work for filming. You can typically earning anywhere from $500 to $5,000 daily. In Ontario, register to host a film shoot with the Ontario Media Development Corporation; in B.C., register with Creative BC.

- **Renting out your place short-term:** Not ready to become a full-time landlord? Short-term rental websites like Airbnb make occasionally renting out your place easier than ever. Help pay for your vacation by renting out your home while you're away, or rent out a spare bedroom during festivals and sporting events, when demand for accommodation is high. If you decide to rent out your place short-term, make sure you aren't breaking any rules. Many cities are cracking down on Airbnb rentals. You'll find more information about Airbnb on my blog.

- **Selling your stuff:** Do some spring cleaning. If you haven't used something in a year—whether it's clothing, electronics, fashion accessories, handbags or movies—consider selling it on eBay. For bigger stuff like furniture and sports equipment, try selling it on Kijiji and Craigslist.

- **Surveys:** Would you like to get paid for sharing your opinion? Give online surveys a shot. They're a great way to make a few bucks here and there. You can sign up for surveys online. My favourites are Legerweb, SurveySavvy and Web Perspectives. You'll find more information about online surveys on my blog.

- **Teaching:** If you have an area of expertise, teach part time with the local school district, or at college or university—or online, for that matter.

- **Virtual assistant:** Help out busy business owners with administrative work such as responding to emails and returning client phone calls.

- **Yardwork:** Mow the lawn and shovel the snow for your neighbours or start your own business.

Acknowledgments

TO JESSE FINKELSTEIN, Megan Jones, Peter Cocking and Zoe Grams of Page Two Strategies, my thanks for your support and guidance in bringing this book to publication. Thanks also to my skilled and patient editor, Judy Phillips.

Sincere thanks goes to Sean Schumacher of Safebridge Financial, Chantel Chapman of Holler for your Dollar and Robert McLister of RateSpy.com for fact-checking the mortgage chapters and the math. And thanks to Kim Leggat, Kristina Wilson, Andrew Kinnaird, Seun Adeyemi of SA Capital and Jason Heath of Objective Financial Partners for their fact-checking.

I'm grateful, too, to Lisa Mehan, Violetta Nadtochyy, Mai Habib, Mudar Badran, Matthew Yantha, Penelope Graham and Jahnome McEwan for their invaluable feedback on an early draft of this book.

To my mother, Maureen Cooper; my father, Richard Cooper; my stepmother, Petra Asfaw; and my sisters, Saba Asfaw and Laura Cooper, thank you for believing in me.

Thank you, Gilbert Wong, for helping me secure the venue for my mortgage-burning party; Eunice Huot, Niruja Sivaguganathan and Evam Gohoho, for helping me organize it; and Sophia Harris, for filming my big moment.

I'd also like to acknowledge my supportive author network. A special thank you to Lesley-Anne Scorgie, Robin R. Speziale and Bruce Sellery. Thanks also to Robert R. Brown, Talbot Stevens, David Chilton, Kyle Prevost, Jonathan Chevreau and Preet Banerjee.

And finally, thank you, Joseph Parsons, for your skillful web design.

Notes

Introduction

1   John Gray (producer), "Trudeau: Hot Housing Sector 'A Real Drag' on Canada's Economy," BNN News, June 9, 2016, http://www.bnn.ca/News/.

2   Tess Kalinowski, "Two-Thirds of Millennials Expect to Afford a Toronto-Area Home, Study Suggests," *Toronto Star*, April 13, 2016, https://www.thestar.com/business.

3   Craig Wong, Canadian Press, "Canadian Delinquency Rate Lowest in More Than 6 Years," *MoneySense*, December 2, 2015, http://www.moneysense.ca/.

Chapter 1

1   Suzanne Fontaine, "Plan for Success in 2015," ProActive Pathways Consulting Inc., March 17, 2015, http://www.proactivepathways.com/.

2   "Take Charge of Saving in Your 40s," *Solutions for Financial Planning*, Winter 2015/2016.

Chapter 2

1   Stacey Bumpus, "Dan Marino and 78 Percent of NFL Players Are Bankrupt or Broke," GOBankingRates, January 30, 2015, http://www.gobankingrates.com/.

2   Blake Morgan, "No Ownership, No Problem: Why Millennials Value Experiences Over Owning Things," *Forbes*, June 1, 2015, http://www.forbes.com/sites/blakemorgan/.

3   Canadian Press, "Most Millennials Consider Home Ownership Important: CIBC Poll," Huffington Post Canada, March 25, 2016, http://www.huffingtonpost.ca/.

4   Canadian Press, "Canada's Debt-to-Income Ratio Sets New Record High at 165%," CBC News, March 11, 2016, http://www.cbc.ca/news/.

5   Jacob Poushter, "3. Social Networking Very Popular among Adult Internet Users in Emerging and Developing Nations," Pew Research Center, February 22, 2016, http://www.pewglobal.org/.

6   Andrew Seale, "FOMO! Millennials Overspending Thanks to Social Media,"
     Yahoo! Finance Canada, March 11, 2015, https://ca.finance.yahoo.com/blogs/
     insight/.

7   "A Map and Table Comparing Cigarette Prices in Canada," Non-Smokers'
     Rights Association, April 9, 2015, http://www.nsra-adnf.ca/cms/.

8   "Gym Membership Statistics," Statistic Brain, December 1, 2015, http://www.
     statisticbrain.com/.

9   David Shum, "Price of Beer at Blue Jays Games 7th Highest in the League:
     Study," Globalnews.ca, July 23, 2015, http://globalnews.ca/news/.

10   This worksheet was inspired by David Bach's *Start Late, Finish Rich* (Toronto:
     Doubleday Canada, 2005).

Chapter 3

1   CNW, "More Than 70 Per Cent of Canadians Ready to Go 'Cashless,'" CNW,
     June 13, 2012, http://www.newswire.ca/news-releases/.

2   "Statistics on Payment, Clearing and Settlement Systems in the CPMI
     Countries—Figures for 2014," n.d., Committee on Payments and Market
     Infrastructures, Bank for International Settlements, December 2015, http://
     www.bis.org/cpmi/publ/d142.pdf.

3   "Credit Cards: Statistics and Facts," Canadian Bankers Association, July 30,
     2015, http://www.cba.ca/en/media-room/.

4   "TransUnion: Canadian Consumers Continue Stable Performance on Credit
     Products," Marketwired, November 18, 2015, http://www.marketwired.com/
     press-release/.

5   "BMO Poll: Nearly Half of Canadian Credit Card Holders Currently Hold
     Credit Card Debt," BMO Financial Group, February 10, 2015, https://
     newsroom.bmo.com/press-releases/.

6   Lindsay Konsko, "Credit Cards Make You Spend More: Studies," NerdWallet,
     July 8, 2014, https://www.nerdwallet.com/blog/.

7   Linda Nguyen, "Top Reason for Divorce? Money, Says BMO Poll," Globalnews.
     ca, February 12, 2014, http://globalnews.ca/news/.

8   Manisha Krishnan, "Canadians Less Satisfied with Banks: Survey," *Toronto
     Star*, July 30, 2015, http://www.thestar.com/business/.

Chapter 4

1   Elisabeth Leamy and Vanessa Weber, "Supermarket Scanner Errors Can Cost
     Consumers up to $2.5 Billion Each Year," ABC News, September 13, 2010,
     http://abcnews.go.com/GMA/ConsumerNews/.

2   Penelope Graham, "The Cost of Love in Canada: $61,821.60," *MoneyWise*,
     February 7, 2016, https://www.ratesupermarket.ca/blog/.

3   Linda Nguyen, "Are You Average? This Is What First-Time Home Buyers Look
     Like in Canada," *Globe and Mail*, April 9, 2013, http://www.theglobeandmail.
     com/globe-investor/.

4   Garry Marr, "Wealthy Canadians Spend Big on Vacations, but Skimp on Flights, Hotels," *Financial Post*, July 2, 2015, http://business.financialpost.com/.

Chapter 5

1   "Help End Food Waste," David Suzuki Foundation, n.d., http://www.davidsuzuki.org/.
2   Canadian Press, "16% of Canadians Watch No Cable TV," CBC News, July 12, 2013, http://www.cbc.ca/news/.
3   Sophia Harris, "Cable Cord-Cutting Numbers Soar in Canada Thanks to Netflix, High Prices, Says Report," CBC News, April 8, 2016, http://www.cbc.ca/news/.
4   Adam Mayers, "Like the Idea of Over-the-Air TV? Here's How to Get Going: Mayers," *Toronto Star*, February 4, 2015, https://www.thestar.com/business/.
5   "CRTC Report Shows More Canadians Going Mobile," CBC News, October 27, 2015, http://www.cbc.ca/news/.
6   Peter Nowak, "Internet, Phone Bills in Canada Too High, Says Consumer Study," CBC News, March 23, 2015, http://www.cbc.ca/news/.

Chapter 6

1   Garry Marr, "Canadians Don't Just Love Home Ownership—They're Growing Fond of Income Properties, Too," *Financial Post*, January 26, 2015, http://business.financialpost.com/personal-finance/.
2   Lisa Wright, "Canadians' Monthly Car Bill: $437.48," *Toronto Star*, July 8, 2014, http://www.thestar.com/business/.
3   Ron Lieber, "Paying Tribute to Thomas Stanley and His 'Millionaire Next Door,'" *New York Times*, March 6, 2015, http://www.nytimes.com/.

Chapter 7

1   Charlie Gillis, Chris Sorensen and Nancy Macdonald, "China Is Buying Canada: Inside the New Real Estate Frenzy," Macleans.ca, May 9, 2016, http://www.macleans.ca/economy/.
2   Adam Mayers, "Emotions Can Run High When Helping the Kids Buy a House: Mayers," *Toronto Star*, June 12, 2015, https://www.thestar.com/business/.
3   Garry Marr, "Inheritance Doesn't Have to Wait," *Financial Post*, October 29, 2011, http://business.financialpost.com/personal-finance/.
4   Alexandra Posadzki, "High Housing Prices Forcing Young Canadians to Team Up with Friends, Family," Huffington Post Canada, April 26, 2016, http://www.huffingtonpost.ca/.

Chapter 9

1   Susan Pigg, "Race to Rhodes Ave.," *Toronto Star*, n.d., http://projects.thestar.com/.

Chapter 10

1   Tania Kohut, "Tips to Iron Out Bad Habits and Improve Your Credit Score," Globalnews.ca, February 26, 2016, http://globalnews.ca/news/.

2   "Do Women Pay More for Mortgages?" Golden Girl Finance, September 11, 2012, http://www.goldengirlfinance.ca/mortgages101/.

3   Will Dunning, "Annual State of the Residential Mortgage Market," Mortgage Professionals Canada, December 2015, http://caamp.org/meloncms/media/Res_Mtge_Mkt_Fall%20Report%20Final.pdf.

4   Rob Carrick, "The Hidden Trap of Mortgage Penalties," *Globe and Mail*, December 5, 2013, http://www.theglobeandmail.com/globe-investor/.

5   Jason Heath, "The Upside of Higher Rates," *Financial Post*, March 31, 2012, http://business.financialpost.com/personal-finance/.

Chapter 11

1   Marie Alcober, "'HGTV' Effect Causes Record Home Renovations," BNN News, July 2, 2014, http://www.bnn.ca/News/.

2   Garry Marr, "'HGTV Effect' Pushes Home Renovation Spending to Record $63-Billion," *Financial Post*, June 30, 2014, http://business.financialpost.com/personal-finance/.

3   "Adding Value with Home Renovations," Get Smarter about Money, http://www.getsmarteraboutmoney.ca/en/managing-your-money/investing/.

4   Anne Bokma, "Why You Should Use a Mortgage Broker," *Canadian Living*, n.d., http://www.canadianliving.com/life/money/6_tips_to_help_you_renew_your_mortgage_2.php.

5   Adam Mayers, "How You Might Save Thousands on Your Mortgage Renewal," *Toronto Star*, May 25, 2014, http://www.thestar.com/business/.

Chapter 13

1   *A Guide to Disability Insurance*, Canadian Life and Health Insurance Association Inc., https://www.clhia.ca/domino/html/clhia/clhia_lp4w_lnd_webstation.nsf/resources/consumer+brochures/$file/brochure_guide_to_disability_eng.pdf.

2   "Divorce Cases in Civil Court, 2010/2011," Statistics Canada, 2012, http://www.statcan.gc.ca/pub/.

3   "Survey: More Than Half of Canadians Do Not Have a Signed Will," LawPro, May 7, 2012, https://www.lawpro.ca/news/pdf/Wills-POAsurvey.pdf.

Index of Key Terms

mortgage penalties, 134–36
moving, 159–62

net worth, 24–26

offer (to purchase), 110–14
open houses and showings, 109–10

payment frequency, 141–42
portability (mortgage), 136
power of attorney and living will, 177
pre-approval (mortgage), 126–28
prepayment privileges (mortgage), 136
pre-qualification (mortgage), 126

rate hold (mortgage), 127
real estate agent, 90–93
refinancing (mortgage), 143–44
Registered Retirement Savings Plan (RRSP). *See* Home Buyers' Plan (HBP)

renewal (mortgage), 149–50
rental ads, 184–86
roommates, 181–82

self-employment and mortgages, 128
showings and open houses, 109–10
SMART goals, 14–15
standard and collateral charges, 136–37

tax-free savings account (TFSA), 79
tenants in common vs. joint tenants, 176
travelling, 52–53

variable-rate mortgage, 138

weddings, 51
will, 175–76

About the Author

SEAN COOPER is a Toronto-based personal finance journalist, money coach, in-demand speaker and author. His articles have been featured in major publications, including the *Toronto Star*, the *Globe and Mail* and *MoneySense*, and he's appeared on Global News, CBC, CP24 and CTV News Network. A senior pension analyst at a global consulting firm, Sean is also mortgage-free, having paid off his mortgage in just three years, by the age of 30.

Follow him on Twitter @SeanCooperWrite

Email him at SeanCooperWriter@gmail.com

Visit his website at www.SeanCooperWriter.com to read his blog, learn more about his services, and to download all worksheets from this book.